Praise for *Work Life Balance Survival Guide*

*"An inspiring 'how to' guide book to help you set up
and live your best life."*

—Shannah Kennedy, master life strategist and bestselling author

"The first part of having a work-life balance is buying this book."
—Josh Zimmerman PCC, founder of Creator Coach®

Praise for *The High School Survival Guide*

*"This book is everything I wish I knew when I was in high school—told
to me by the mentor I wish I had! Every student should be armed with
Jess' guide."*

—Pritish Agarwal, partner manager, YouTube

*"High School Survival Guide teaches you how to survive both school and
life! The emphasis on passion, organization, balance, and discipline are
themes throughout the book, but also the TRUE keys to success in life."*

—Lenoria Addison, partner manager, AwesomenessTV

*"Don't we all need a Jessica in our lives? She's that friend who not
only motivates you but makes things seem much less daunting. This is
a really sweet, encouraging handbook to have during a time when
we all need that extra motivation and support."*

—Natalie Tran, The Community Channel

T0035156

Work Life Balance
Survival Guide

Other books by Jessica Holsman

The High School Survival Guide:
Your Roadmap to Studying, Socializing, and Succeeding

Work Life
Balance
SURVIVAL GUIDE

How to Find
Your Flow State
and Create a
Life of Success

JESSICA HOLSMAN
from *Study with Jess*

mango
PUBLISHING GROUP

For permission requests, please contact the publisher at:
Mango Publishing Group
2850 S Douglas Road, 4th Floor
Coral Gables, FL 33134 USA
info@mango.bz

For special orders, quantity sales, course adoptions and corporate sales, please email the publisher at sales@mango.bz. For trade and wholesale sales, please contact Ingram Publisher Services at customer.service@ingramcontent.com or +1.800.509.4887.

Work Life Balance Survival Guide: How to Find Your Flow State and Create a Life of Success

Library of Congress Cataloging-in-Publication number: 2022937644
ISBN: (print) 978-1-64250-952-6, (ebook) 978-1-64250-953-3
BISAC category code SEL035000, SELF-HELP / Self-Management / Time Management

Printed in the United States of America

To my amazing husband, Adam. Thank you for supporting me in everything I do. Your unconditional love and ongoing encouragement empower me to be the best possible version of myself. I love you.

"It is not enough to be busy, so are the ants. The question is what are you so busy about?"

—Henry David Thoreau

Table of Contents

My Story

It's been seven years since I graduated from university with a postgraduate diploma in psychology and decided to leave behind my volunteer job as a crisis telephone counsellor and anxiety support group facilitator, and a full scholarship to commence a PhD, studying childhood neurodevelopmental disorders. Instead, I took a leap of faith and honoured my calling to help people in a way that was authentic to me by starting my own business and YouTube channel, *Study With Jess*. Through the lens of the perceived societal expectations that I grew up in, it could be seen as quite the shocking career pivot. "She gave up a PhD to become a YouTuber!?" Putting my inner critic and her unhelpful judgements back in the box where she belongs, I can now say that it was the best, most challenging, and fulfilling decision I've made in my career.

Since launching my channel and establishing my career online, my channel has received more than 27 million views. I am continually grateful for the opportunity to harness the power of social media to help my community increase their productivity, boost their mental health, stress less, and bring about long-lasting success. My intention has always been to help people live a happy, healthy, and productive life, so being able to engage with my online community and hear how my work supports, inspires, comforts, and motivates people fills me with a deeply satisfying level of fulfilment and gratitude. Building an online community of like-minded people who strive for self-improvement has also given me the platform to launch my business Educationery, the first-ever study stationery line for students. While the process initially began with sketching my numerous ideas for designs while in bed, sometimes until as late as 3:00 a.m., the line has since expanded and now consists of paper-based and digital study planners. Each planner's template helps students plan out major assignments and homework, as well as study for exams effectively to avoid last-minute cramming and any unnecessary added stress.

A career in social media never crossed my mind until my mid-twenties. This initially unconventional career path has been full of exciting opportunities and avenues for spreading my message and bringing more light into the world through educational, creative, and entertaining content. I've partnered with organisations, including Google and Screen Australia, to create two web series, *Life of Jess* and *MindFull*. I have also had the pleasure of working alongside globally renowned brands whose values align with mine, including Netflix, Adobe, ASUS, and Microsoft. And of course, I've had the pleasure of authoring my first book, *The High School Survival Guide*, which has since become a bestseller and includes many of the lessons I acquired throughout school, university, and later, while building my business.

My vibrant career has required me to further flex my productivity and planning muscles (although I have always been quite the planner addict) to develop an optimal schedule and lifestyle that supports my needs. It has taught me the importance of living intentionally, frequently being the editor of my own life—my schedule, priorities, and commitments, and getting clear on what a successful and sustainable life looks like. It's also taught me about the interconnection between productivity and work-life balance. In fact, it's made me re-

evaluate my understanding of work-life balance and the importance it plays in all areas of my life, not just in my career.

Welcome

It's been a minute since I released my first book, *The High School Survival Guide*, and while it feels like a while ago, I always knew there would come a time when inspiration would strike and my love for writing and creating would lead me to author a second book. My family and I still laugh when we think about the fact that as a young child, my mother would have to incentivise me to read by any means possible, buying fashion magazines from the supermarket hoping that I would read some of the articles as I flipped through the pages. Let's also not forget when I wrote an entire book report in eighth grade and received an A+ for my assignment, despite the book never existing. Credit goes to my wild imagination and ability to craft a detailed report to make it look as though I had read a book outside of the school syllabus that year! Nowadays, I practically inhale books (mostly self-development and business), and my husband can't believe the rate I move through them—I occasionally finish two or three per week, especially when I was researching for this book. I think I have always harboured a love for reading and writing but I won't just read anything. I need to be fully invested in whichever book I pick up and see how it can add value to my life. It needs to inspire me, support me, leave me feeling empowered, open my eyes to new ways of thinking, or comfort me when I feel stressed, lost, or overwhelmed. I knew I wanted my next book to do just that for my readers. I couldn't write a second book simply for the sake of writing a second book. Everything I do must come from a place of intention and love, so that whatever I put out into the world can have the greatest impact possible.

Preface

The story of how this book came to fruition could be seen as one of serendipity or perhaps synchronicity. I am often one of the first to arrive to my yoga classes because I like to plan for any unexpected traffic and I think that the idea of rushing to get to yoga when the intention is to finally relax seems counterproductive. I was the first to arrive at class that day, pushing open the bright yellow wooden door to find my yoga teacher Pru, standing behind the desk wearing her friendly smile and looking particularly energised for a Thursday morning. As I said good morning, she responded with, "I didn't know that you're *Study With Jess*! I saw your posts online and I said to myself, 'I just *have* to talk to Jess!' Every time I sit down to work on my thesis, I can't help but end up staring at the wall."

After being away from university for twenty years, starting a family and setting up the yoga studio, Pru was studying for a master's degree and finding it hard to focus, feel motivated, and get her work done. Her challenges were not unlike many of my online community. I told her how nice it was to hear she liked my work, before another person walked in the door to sign in for class. I went through to the studio and rolled out my new blue yoga mat with a mandala design and lay down to meditate before class started. Two poses into the class and my mind continued to think and chatter away. I thought to myself as I stared up at one of the many skylights above my head, *How am I going to help Pru? And how am I going to help everyone else in my online community who's experiencing the same*

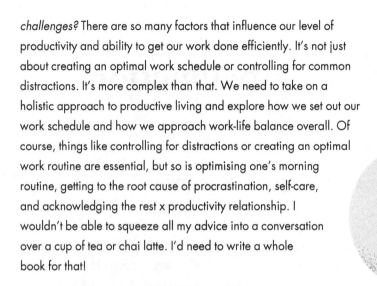

challenges? There are so many factors that influence our level of productivity and ability to get our work done efficiently. It's not just about creating an optimal work schedule or controlling for common distractions. It's more complex than that. We need to take on a holistic approach to productive living and explore how we set out our work schedule and how we approach work-life balance overall. Of course, things like controlling for distractions or creating an optimal work routine are essential, but so is optimising one's morning routine, getting to the root cause of procrastination, self-care, and acknowledging the rest x productivity relationship. I wouldn't be able to squeeze all my advice into a conversation over a cup of tea or chai latte. I'd need to write a whole book for that!

This book is an example of how just a one-minute conversation about the struggles of sitting down to work can plant a seed of inspiration and grow into an entirely new resource for the world. Too often we forget how powerful a short exchange between two people can be.

Experiences and encounters like these make me believe there is always a spark of inspiration within us, waiting for the right time to be ignited. And when that time comes, when that ah-ha moment finally happens, and we feel that passion inside us come alive, it's our duty to feel into it, honour it, and trust that we are being guided and steered in the right direction.

Introduction

Planning for Success

Just as I am intentional with the work that I commit to, so is my approach to getting my work done and setting out my days. I'm a huge advocate for planning, but I understand that plans are not rules. Plans are better than rules. Plans are guides that still leave room for flexibility. I have always been a planner, for as long as I can remember. Back in my university days, I used to sit in the library upstairs where it was quiet and plan out my study schedule for the week. I would block out when I would revise my notes, work on assignments, or study for exams. It gave me the structure I needed to feel more in control of my life. Rewinding a little further back into my high school years, I would decorate my school diary with pride and write down any assignment due dates the moment the teacher would tell us. Jumping back to today, I have a collection of planners to cater to all my planning needs, from a yearly planner to help me space out and schedule my work for writing this book and meeting the ambitious deadline (which we then moved up!), to daily and weekly planners for keeping me on track with short-term projects and commitments, and my precious diary that is the gatekeeper of how I best spend my time and make sure I don't neglect my own needs.

As you make your way through this book, you'll see that planning is a key part of creating the necessary framework for productivity and practising the philosophy of work-life balance. I equate planning to intentional living and believe it forms the foundation for a fulfilling and successful life by assisting us to use our time wisely. Evidently, time is one of our most valuable assets. It's what we want more of but often use most poorly. I love planning because it has helped me in numerous ways:

* Planning maximises your precious time and leaves little room for procrastination and other time-wasters

* Planning helps direct your attention to your top priorities (work, relationships, and wellbeing)

* Planning reduces stress and overwhelm because everything is accounted for in your schedule

How to Use this Book

This book is for you if:

* You've ever found yourself lacking motivation, staring at a blank wall, and struggling to be productive.

* You've felt lost, unmotivated, or lacking structure in your days but don't know how to get your life back on track and regain a sense of control.

* You've experienced burnout, exhaustion, or brain fog and have felt stressed or overwhelmed by your growing to-do list and jam-packed schedule.

* You want to increase your productivity and focus, optimise your days, and enhance your wellbeing and mental fitness.

This book is more than just about finding a better work-life balance. It's designed to help you increase your productivity, take back control of life's many distractions, maximise your precious time, and increase your level of personal satisfaction. And because productivity and wellbeing are intertwined—as you'll soon see— the advice and strategic exercises throughout this book are designed to help you prevent burnout, reduce anxiety, stress, and overwhelm, and create a more sustainable and supportive lifestyle where you can still get everything done that's *truly* important to you.

Whether you're currently studying or have entered the workforce, this book will help you spend your time more wisely when it comes to your work and personal life. I'll share with you how to maximise your productivity for efficient and deeply focused work while still making time for yourself to create a life that supports your needs, aligns with your goals, and is driven by your desires.

The ideas and exercises found throughout this book are strategically set out so that each chapter builds on the concepts outlined before, creating an easy-to-follow step-by-step framework for helping you to maximise your overall level of productivity and enhance your wellbeing. It's your guide on finding your flow state and getting the important things done without getting overwhelmed!

To help you get acquainted with the concepts and exercises to come, I've divided this book into five sections:

1. Planning Your Day for Success
2. Finding Your Flow
3. Barriers to Flow
4. Achieving Better Work-Life Balance
5. Reset for a New Week

The first section is designed to help you plan out your days. I'll begin by helping you establish a successful morning routine to create a strong foundation for your day. We'll then work together to create the optimal work schedule that will give you the necessary structure each day to get your work done while controlling any distractions and ensuring you don't feel overwhelmed. This will be your framework for productive living and help you spend your time wisely to feel energised and focused throughout the day.

The next section, Part 2, is all about finding your flow and getting into the "work zone," where we are our most productive and accomplish deep work. You'll discover numerous ways to help you enter this place of least resistance, where time can appear to fly by, and you find yourself in this state of momentum. From creating the optimal work environment to offering powerful, effective, yet easy to implement rituals that can fast track this process, this section of the book is what has helped me to get my best work done and I'm confident it will do the same for you!

We'll then move on to Part 3 of this book, where I help you overcome the many obstacles that can pull you away from this place of deep focus and productivity and can eat into your precious time off. While many books on work-life balance emphasise the importance of self-care, I've yet to come across one that gives examples of how to nurture yourself *and* successfully create time in your day for these practices while acknowledging our busy lives. This is why the first portion of this book is specifically designed to help you maximise your efficiency while you work, so that you *can* create more space in your day for yourself. I believe that in this busy age, to have sufficient time off (and to fully enjoy it) requires you to work at your most efficient and productive level. This is why we'll also cover issues in this section like procrastination and distractions that, if otherwise left unaddressed, can cause significant anxiety and stress and eat into your precious "you" time. My intention for you as you enter this third section is to feel empowered and armed to take back control of how you spend your time and attention.

In Part 4, it's time to take a holistic look at what it truly means to be productive and how you can achieve a better work-life balance *without* experiencing burnout. It's time to begin putting yourself first. I'll take you through my favourite self-care practices and habits to help spark inspiration. This is also where I propose a new term or concept to encourage you to adopt a new way of thinking about your work and personal needs. You'll discover how to once and for all successfully allocate your time and energy and integrate the many aspects that make up your wonderful life.

The book concludes with my guided formula for another successful day and week. By now you will have created your optimal morning routine, so it's time to bookend your day—how you end your day is just as important as how you choose to begin. I'll then take you through a powerful end-of-week reflection exercise to help you plan for another successful, productive, and intentional week ahead. Finally, because life is unpredictable and we are all human, I leave you with my advice on how to best navigate any bumps in the road that might steer you off track.

Before We Begin...

I want to preface by saying that I don't expect perfection because that's just not who I am, and this book is not designed to set you up for failure. So when those bumps appear in the road—*when*, not *if*, you encounter a hiccup or life happens and you veer off track—I'm going to show you how to get back on track sooner and with a greater level of ease so that you can keep moving forward. Contrary to how society has painted life to be a game of competition and one of winners and losers, life is not like a game of *Mario Kart*, where if you fall off track and into the abyss, you commence back at the start. There is no such thing as failure in my world and I invite you to disregard this concept completely and adopt a growth mindset instead. This work is about constantly moving forward with greater awareness and being the editor of your life. It's about knowing that with each bump in the road, you will find yourself better equipped to move back into alignment and protect your wellbeing. Importantly, you'll do it with greater self-compassion, awareness, and intention. Your bump in the road might involve working through anxiety, grief, illness, navigating a pandemic, or any other unexpected responsibilities that take precedence over your initial plans. Whatever it is, please remember to be kind to yourself. Be gentle with yourself. Acknowledge that you are human and know that we are all doing the best we can.

As someone who has grappled with perfection and spent a lot of time talking to my psychologist and life coach to free myself from these chains I used to place around my neck (metaphorically speaking), I want to emphasise that this book is not here to advocate for a perfect life, a perfect routine, or a perfect plan 100 percent of the time. Because perfection is unsustainable and unrealistic and I wouldn't be doing my job properly if I didn't acknowledge that we are all human beings, life happens, and you need to take this into account. I expect you will have to steer your ship during a storm or two throughout the years, which is why I choose to acknowledge this and will also share with you my numerous tools and strategies to help you navigate these challenges and feel supported along the way. This book is a realistic

and sustainable approach to productivity, wellbeing, and work-
life balance. It's here to guide you and provide you with the
necessary framework to feel in control of your life so that you
can achieve your goals. Importantly, this is a guidebook, not a
rulebook. You can always reschedule, edit, and revise in life, but
the framework itself is what's most important.

Ready? Let's begin!

PART 1:

Planning Your Day for Success

CHAPTER 1:

Optimising Your Mornings

"I love the smell of possibility in the morning."

–Anonymous

This chapter was a no-brainer for me when planning this book. I knew I needed to include a chapter that not only talks about the importance of forming an optimal morning routine but helps you take actionable steps to form your own successful routine. I am a huge advocate for having a great morning routine because it is essential to our overall productivity and is a pillar in striving for, if not maintaining, work-life balance, as you'll soon see. I understand that not everyone considers themselves to be a morning person. Some of us naturally feel more alert first thing in the morning and ready to take on the day. Others consider themselves more like night owls. While I consider myself to be an early bird whose mind naturally wakes as the sun rises and simultaneously clocks off as it begins to set, my morning routine has not come naturally to me. Even us early risers need a framework for how to start our mornings optimally! This chapter is designed to help you, regardless of whether you are naturally a morning person or someone who reluctantly hits snooze multiple times before shuffling to the kitchen to make a cup of coffee to mentally prepare you for human interaction and tackling to-do lists. You don't have to love mornings but embracing them will have great benefits for the rest of your day. As Tim Ferris, bestselling author of *The 4-Hour Work Week*, says, "If you win the morning, you win the day."

I never truly appreciated the importance of having a morning routine, let alone a successfully optimised and mindful one, until I had repeatedly experienced burnout in the first two years of starting my business. As a student, I had never acknowledged the rhythm and flow that formed the basis of my morning habits and daily "getting ready" activities. I took my morning routine that had become automated over the years for granted. Since graduating from high school and, later, university, I no longer had a strict start time to my day. My morning movements were no longer dictated by my class schedule, and I was now in charge of how I organised and spent my time. Being my own boss, coupled with the ease of accessibility of my work, thanks to everything now being online, meant that I had to exercise some serious self-discipline and figure out how to begin my days in a more efficient and healthy way. With my newfound sense of freedom, I developed some unhealthy habits, such as reaching for my phone upon waking to check whether any new overseas emails had come through from the US. Each morning, I would hit the ground running (with work rather than exercise) and my adrenaline and cortisol levels had no choice but to try and keep up with my go-getter tendencies, that is, until they couldn't. My mornings lacked structure, and too often, I would prioritise work, leaving my personal needs fighting for any gaps of "spare" time in my day.

Enter: Josh Zimmerman, my life coach, who has since drilled into me the importance of an optimal morning routine and turned me into an advocate for ensuring that the first hour of our day is used for prioritising our wellbeing. Your morning routine should prime you into a state of readiness for the day, so it's essential to use this time wisely and be as intentional as you can so you can reap the benefits. I've learned that if something is important to you, it needs to be prioritised first thing; otherwise, it's left to compete for your attention (often unsuccessfully) with whatever tasks might be left on your to-do list or unexpected urgencies that pop up throughout the day.

I understand that not everyone needs a morning routine to save them from their overworking tendencies. While I initially needed to make some drastic and necessary adjustments to my morning routine for this reason, I've also experienced the opposite. During the pandemic of 2020 and later, in 2021, my state experienced three extended lockdowns. As day one blurred into day thirty, then sixty, and then ninety, I felt my motivation begin to fall. I started waking up progressively later, skipping my morning workouts and meditation, feeling too uninspired to work, and grieving for my old life. I sat with my feelings, and after letting myself feel sad, angry, unmotivated, tired, and emotionally heavy for a few more days, I knew I needed to reach out for help and implement some changes to once again redesign my morning routine and help get my life back on track. I immediately began to feel better as I incorporated little rituals and formed new and healthier habits, like waking up at 7:30 a.m., meditating for five to ten minutes, making the bed, doing a little skincare routine, and choosing an online yoga or Pilates class several mornings a week. It might sound simple, but at the time, my mental health, like many others, was hanging on tight to these little rituals. It gave me the structure and control I was craving, so I wouldn't feel all over the place. The pandemic took a huge toll on all our lives. Our schedules and routines were either shaken up or virtually thrown out

the window for a while. I received a lot of messages from my online community during this time as well. People shared with me that their motivation was lacking, and they felt depressed, anxious, lost, stressed out, burnt out, overwhelmed, or like their entire life was out of control. In addition to having amazing professional support and keeping in touch with my psychologist, I shared how a successful morning routine managed to give me back a sense of control, stability, structure, and a way to embed more self-care into my day. I know it isn't the cure for a lot of these problems, but it can have an enormous influence on our days and be the difference between starting the day off feeling anxious or lost versus beginning a new day feeling like our feet are on solid ground.

Creating a mindful morning routine brings many benefits. It sets you up for a successful day ahead by helping you to ease into the day, prioritise your wellbeing first thing, increase your focus to help make better decisions, and program your mind for positivity and possibility, which is vital no matter who you are or what you're up against. There's a reason Robin Sharma, bestselling author of *The Monk Who Sold His Ferrari* and *The 5 AM Club*, calls the first thirty minutes of your day your "Platinum 30," because they are the most valuable moments of your day and greatly influence the quality of each minute and hour that follows. He even goes on to liken it to a basecamp, where to climb the mountain and scale the summit, you need to have a good basecamp that provides a sanctuary for rest, renewal, and replenishing. This is like a morning routine that offers a daily opportunity to re-energise, renew ourselves, and refocus on what is most important to us.

Even the seemingly simple act of making one's bed first thing in the morning can have a powerful and influential effect on how your day plays out. While making your bed acts as a physical deterrent to retreating under the covers, it also eases you into an action state from the beginning of the day. Choosing for this to be the first thing you do each morning also provides a sense of accomplishment. In his book *Make Your Bed*, William H. McRaven, a US Navy four-star admiral, talks about the significance of this daily act.

"Making my bed correctly was not going to be an opportunity for praise. It was expected of me. It was my first task of the day, and doing it right was important. It demonstrated my discipline. It showed my attention to detail, and at the end of the day it would be a reminder that I had done something well, something to be proud of, no matter how small the task."

I believe that it isn't the act of making your bed per se that can transform your day. Instead, it's more about the importance of starting your day off with consistency and familiarity and building in opportunities first thing in the day for you to experience elevated emotions like pride, which comes from a feeling of accomplishment, no matter how small the task might be. I also think that our mornings can provide us with even more mental, physical, and emotional benefits, if we effectively prioritise our needs and know how to efficiently utilise this sacred time in our day.

> **"You'll never change your life until you change something you do daily. The secret of your success is found in your daily routine."**

–John C. Maxwell

I've read that the world's most successful businesspeople all have at least one thing in common—how they prioritise their morning routine and use it to form the foundation for a successful day. Richard Branson gets going at 5:45 a.m. to exercise and have an early breakfast. Oprah Winfrey wakes up alarm-free between 6:02 and 6:20 a.m. before prioritising meditation and nature every morning. Ariana Huffington begins her day with twenty to thirty minutes of meditation. Former Disney CEO Robert Iger wakes up at 4:30 a.m. to exercise and read the paper before doing his emails and watching TV.

The importance of a morning routine and its influence on the rest of our day is also highlighted by the sheer number of YouTube videos uploaded daily on this topic. Just a quick search using the keywords "morning routine" on YouTube shows it's one of the most frequently uploaded and most-watched kinds of videos online, and for good reason. My morning routine videos are some of my most-watched pieces of content on YouTube, each acquiring hundreds of thousands of views. From life coaches, psychologists, and bestselling productivity authors to daily vloggers, wellness and lifestyle influencers, mummy vloggers, and fitness creators, people across the globe are sharing their updated morning routines, as our online community desperately tries to figure out how to start their day, hoping their morning routine holds the key to unlocking greater productivity and wellbeing.

Here's a Little Look at My Current Morning Routine:

In the warmer months, my mornings usually start between 7:15 and 7:30 a.m. I've gotten good at waking up with the natural light that peers through our bedroom curtains and beating the alarm on my phone that I leave out of reach and away from my bed. I keep a watch on my bedside table so that I can check the time without relying on my phone. After a few moments spent remembering any vivid dreams from the night before, I carefully get out of bed while trying not to wake our Shih-Tzu cross, Winston, who jumps on the bed by 6:00 a.m. to catch a few extra hours of shuteye at either Adam's or my feet. Once I'm up, I wander over to the bathroom to wash my face, brush my teeth, and do a little skincare routine. I got this idea from a friend of mine who begins her day by saying some positive affirmations to herself in the mirror and adapted it so that with each skincare product, I recite a series of affirmations to myself. It goes like this:

* Cleanser: "I am enough. I love and accept myself exactly as I am"

* Hydrating mist: "I love my body and my body loves me"

* Serum: "I trust in the divine timing of my life"

* Moisturiser: "I am loved, supported, and guided through life"

After I complete my skincare routine, I walk over to the kitchen to make a cup of tea (usually hot water with lemon and honey). Then I take a seat at the dining table with my tea, looking out the window and easing into my day, slowly waking up and reflecting on my gratitudes. This is also around the time when I can hear Winston's little pitter-patter on our hardwood floors. Winsty takes his morning cuddles in the home office on the rug before catching his first wind of energy for the day. It's as if his morning energy pill kicks in at the same precise moment each morning and he is instantly in the mood to play! Our morning routines then blur into one, as he chooses his "morning toy of choice" (currently a plush mini lamb, a.k.a. "Baah Lamb," or squeaky ball) and if weather permits, we go outside to the garden and I throw it around for him to chase and pounce. Once Adam has had his breakfast, he takes Winston on their morning walk, while I use that time to make the bed and complete a short five- to ten-minute guided meditation, unless I plan to attend a yoga class later that morning. I also like to randomly pick an affirmation card from the bowl on the windowsill and use it to guide me throughout the day. My mum used to have a box of affirmation cards with the most beautiful little fairy illustrations and a positive word on each one (such as wisdom, love, joy, grace, and transformation), and I recently rediscovered them in a store a few years back and bought my own. Afterwards, I have a light breakfast and either head to my morning yoga class (and later, the office to work), or opt for an at-home online Pilates workout before sitting down to work by 9:30 a.m.

Notice that there was no mention of checking my phone, responding to text messages, scrolling through social media, or checking the news. This is because your phone is the source of three N's, as bestselling author and wisdom-filled coach Jay Shetty explains. The 3 N's refer to noise, negativity, and news—three big distractions that pull your attention away from what's most important and can negatively impact your mood and focus before your day has begun to unfold. While news is self-explanatory, *noise* can be anything that unnecessarily takes up space in your mind, such as online advertisements, other people's social media posts and videos, or clickbaity articles about celebrity couples or fashion faux pas.

Negativity, on the other hand, could be content that triggers self-comparison or feelings of lack (often due to curated social media content) or, more often than not, comes from the stories we discover while reading the news and are designed to elicit fear or sadness. I can't stress this enough. Please, *please* limit your technology usage in the mornings, ideally for the first hour or at least for the first thirty minutes of the day. According to a research study from IDC that surveyed eighteen- to forty-four-year-old iPhone and Android smartphone owners in the US, about 80 percent were found to check their mobile phones within the first fifteen minutes of waking each morning. The negative implications of this behaviour are evident. Wellbeing expert Chelsea Pottenger surveyed 95,000 people over three years to understand what effect this behaviour had on mental and emotional health. She found that the act of checking your phone jolts our brain into a wave of high stress from the moment we wake up, causing feelings of worry, anger, irritability, and paranoia—all of which are linked to having a weaker immune system. That's enough for me to steer clear of my phone for the first hour every day.

An Activity to Spark Greater Self-awareness:

To bring your current morning routine habits into view, write down all your habits (both healthy and unhealthy) that currently make it into your mornings. Making a list of your daily activities helps you to become conscious of your habits. For example, your list might look like this:

1. Hit snooze

2. Wake up

3. Get out of bed

4. Use the bathroom

5. Brush teeth

6. Make coffee

7. Make the bed

8. Read the news

9. Make breakfast

10. Take a shower

_____

_____

_____

_____

Next, determine which habits serve you, hurt you, or are neutral by sorting them into three categories in the following table.

To help you decide whether a habit is helpful, consider which of these habits contribute to your overall wellbeing, productivity, and focus throughout the day. Helpful habits should leave you feeling grateful, happy, optimistic, calm, centred, energised, or focused.

Harmful habits, on the other hand, negatively impact your overall wellbeing, productivity, and focus throughout the day. They might leave you feeling wired, stressed, overwhelmed, distracted, ungrateful, sad, or perhaps mentally or emotionally drained before the day has started.

Neutral habits are acts that simply need to get done but doing them doesn't directly impact your mood or focus, such as brushing your teeth or going to the bathroom.

Helpful Habits	Harmful Habits	Neutral Habits

What sort of changes or boundaries can you put into place to best support you in removing these harmful habits from your mornings? Use the following table to brainstorm potential solutions.

Here are a couple of examples to help you:

* Say that your negative habit involves checking your phone first thing in the morning and scrolling on social media. One barrier or change you could implement is instead of leaving your phone next to your bed, which acts as a temptation, leave it charging in another room overnight and invest in an alarm clock or leave the blinds up to wake up to natural light. Removing the object from your sight and making it less accessible will remove the external cue (the sight of your phone), making you less likely to reach for it on waking to check your social media feed.

✴ If your bad habit involves staying in your pyjamas for the first few hours of the day (if not the entire day) because you have the freedom of working/studying from home, try setting an alarm each evening to encourage you to lay out your clothes the night before, thereby creating a positive cue to get dressed upon waking.

Harmful Habits	Change/Boundary I Can Implement

> "Depending on what we are, our habits will either make us or break us. We become what we repeatedly do."
>
> –Sean Covey

How Do You R.I.S.E. for the Day?

I created an acronym to help you simplify your morning routine down to the most important elements. I've reduced it to four elements that I encourage you to implement within approximately the first hour, which I believe have the most powerful effect on our days. These four elements are also what have stood out to me when researching the morning routines of some of the world's most successful people and a lot of trial and error on my end to figure out what makes a great morning routine! By prioritising these four things each morning, you are prioritising yourself, and in doing so, you are putting yourself in the best possible position for a productive day ahead. I should also mention that while I have written out these four elements in a particular order, it is simply for ease of remembering them in a helpful acronym. You are welcome to complete each of these four elements in any order that suits you.

R.I.S.E.

* **Ritual:** A morning ritual is an excellent way to ease into the day and it can be any number of different things, depending on what works best for you. Some examples include meditation, mindful breathing, making a cup of tea or morning coffee, the simple act of picking a flower outside, watering the garden, having a skincare routine, or reading a page from a morning meditations book.

* **Intention:** Set a daily intention to ground you for the day ahead before the busyness sets in and pulls your focus. I recommend starting with the words "I am" to anchor your and will it into existence. Here are a few intentions I regularly use: *I am calm, I am centred, I am grounded, I am supported, I am grateful, and I am present, peaceful, patient, and calm.*

* **Sweat/Stretch:** Make sure to move your body and create time to exercise in some form. Even ten or fifteen minutes of exercising before work helps us make better decisions throughout the day because it helps us to think more clearly, boosts creativity, and helps reduce stress. Some mornings I will go to a yoga class or do an online Pilates workout.

Other mornings I take Winston for a walk or run around the backyard with him to help get the "morning sillies" out of his system.

✳ **Exhale:** Anchor yourself in the morning by beginning with a few moments of deep breathing. This could involve taking three deep breaths upon waking or spending five minutes engaging in some mindful breathing while sipping your tea, listening to music, or tuning into guided mindfulness meditation. It's easy for the simple act of breathing to be taken for granted, especially since our bodies are breathing without any effort on our end. I invite you at this moment to direct your attention inwards and notice your breathing. Most of us don't breathe deeply enough throughout the day, despite its many health benefits. Deep breathing helps to tune into our parasympathetic nervous system, which helps restore the body to calm and helps us feel more centred and prepared for the day. It oxygenates our bodies and brains so we can focus and think more clearly. It quiets our minds when we feel anxious, overwhelmed, or stressed.

Remember that your R.I.S.E. will look different from the R.I.S.E. of others. Also, keep in mind that while it's something I recommend you prioritise in the first sixty minutes of your morning, it can be simplified and streamlined to take as little as twenty to thirty minutes. If you're still short on time, I encourage you to wake up a little earlier to make time for yourself.

To demonstrate how your R.I.S.E. can take as little as twenty to thirty minutes, here are two examples you can use as inspiration if you're pressed for time in the mornings. I've written them chronologically to help paint a picture of how to seamlessly integrate them into a morning routine.

Exhale: Begin with three deep breaths upon waking

Intention: Pick an affirmation card and display it on your windowsill to set an intention for the day

Ritual: Make tea/coffee and sip it mindfully

Sweat/Stretch: Take the dog for a walk around the block

Intention: Set an intention upon waking

Sweat/Stretch: Practise a few sun salutations

Exhale: Breathe deeply, pairing each breath with a movement as you practise your sun salutations

Ritual: Stop by your local coffee shop on the way to work to grab your morning coffee

To help you create your optimal morning routine, I've included a list of excellent morning routine habits and categorised them based on their function. You might like to choose a few from the list or come up with more on your own that you'd like to incorporate. Whatever you choose, I encourage you to notice how your day unfolds when you prioritise the things that matter most to you.

Calming Habits	Energising Habits	Healthy Habits
Take three deep breaths	Yoga	Take your vitamins
Pick an affirmation card	Pilates	Make a fresh juice
Herbal tea	Try an online workout	Eat a nutritious breakfast
Water the garden	Walk outside	Rehydrate with a glass of water
Pick a flower	Morning jog/run	
Journal	Stretch	Wake up at the same time each morning
Light a candle	Stand in the morning sunshine	
Diffuse an essential oil		Wake up to natural light (in the summertime)
Read a few pages of a book	Spend five minutes tidying up	
	Make your bed	Avoid technology for the first hour

Joyful Habits	Self-love Habits
Play with a pet	Recite your own positive affirmations in the mirror
Write down three gratitudes	Create a skincare routine
Set a daily intention	Take a hot bath/shower
Listen to upbeat music	Wear your favourite perfume
Listen to a motivational podcast	Try a new heavenly body wash in the shower

A note on habits:

When thinking about the habits you want to form, think about how you want to feel after you've practised each one. Then, decide which habits will give you the desired outcome or feeling. Do you want to feel more calm, energised, or focused? For example, if you want to feel calm in the mornings, brainstorm a list of habits that you could consider building into the first hour of your day to achieve this outcome before selecting the ones that you'd enjoy most and are most confident you could stick with.

An Activity to Spark Action:

Write down which helpful habits you will include in your morning routine. Next to each habit, make a note of how this action makes you feel. For example, taking three deep breaths upon waking might

make you feel calm, or going for a jog might make you feel more alert and energised. Attaching a feeling to each habit helps to build incentive and the motivation to stick to it.

Helpful Habit	Associated Feeling

Now it's time to build out your optimised morning routine. To begin, write down how you intend to R.I.S.E. each morning.

My R.I.S.E.

R: _____

I: _____

S: _____

E: _____

Next, use the space on the next page to schedule your morning routine while including your R.I.S.E. What time do you plan to wake up? Use the timestamps to plan out your morning.

＊   When it comes to habit formation, the act of writing down your
     goals significantly increases your likelihood of accomplishing
     them. By taking a few minutes here to write what your ideal
     morning routine looks like to you, you're increasing your
     chances of successfully implementing these new daily habits.

___*a.m.* _____

___*a.m.* _____

___*a.m.* _____

___*a.m.* _____

___*a.m.* _____

___*a.m.* _____

___*a.m.* _____

___*a.m.* _____

___*a.m.* _____

___*a.m.* _____

To help you stick to your new habits, try utilising helpful cues around
the house to increase your likelihood of committing to each one daily. Here's a list of some simple changes I have made to my environment to eliminate obstacles and introduce new and helpful external
cues that remind me to do the things I *want* to do each day!

＊   I now keep a watch on my bedside table to keep track of
     time in the mornings and reduce the number of reasons for
     checking my phone.

＊   I have placed my earbuds on my desk to remind me to put
     my feet up while I listen to music and do ten minutes of
     deep breathing.

＊   I pick out my clothes the night before and place them on my
     chair so I don't put off getting dressed in the mornings.

＊   I leave my yoga mat in my backyard to encourage me to
     stretch in the morning sunshine.

* I leave my citrus reamer on the kitchen bench to remind me to make fresh orange and lemon juice in the mornings. I also keep my greens powder and bone broth on the bench so I don't forget these either.

A note on flexible work hours:

I acknowledge that due to my work flexibility and the ability to choose when I sit down at my desk, my morning routine is typically longer than an hour. If you find that you do not have enough time to complete all the things you'd like to do each morning, my recommendation would be to try waking up a little earlier so you don't have to sacrifice any of the helpful habits you've chosen to include.

Remember, you get to choose how you start your day, so make sure it's one that works best for you. There's no such thing as *the* perfect morning routine because it's not a one-size-fits-all approach. Experiment with your morning routine, making sure it supports and grounds you for the day ahead.

CHAPTER 2:

Creating Your Optimal Work Schedule

"Don't confuse activity with productivity. Many people are simply busy being busy."

–Robin Sharma

Now that you've equipped yourself with a morning routine designed to give you some much-needed structure and self-care to begin your day, it's time to think about the remaining hours of your day. Much like how your morning routine provides you with the necessary structure to best make use of your initial waking hours, an optimised work schedule will help to create a plan for how to intentionally and wisely use the hours that follow.

The problem is most people spend their day in a state of reaction rather than intention. They hand over their control to their external environment and everything that's happening around them by reacting to messages, emails, phone calls, and requests or tasks that pop up throughout the day. There's never going to be a shortage

of distractions or last-minute tasks that mask themselves as urgent, but these imposter priorities and temptations can often sabotage our days and end up leaving us feeling like we've failed to get our best work done. To put it simply, most people are busy being busy. They are not advancing towards their goals because they are spending their time reacting to other people's priorities or they are too focused on unimportant tasks. I'll offer myself as an example. In the past, I used to get so caught up with what everyone else on social media was doing. Before another one of my sessions with my life/business coach, I wrote down an entire list of everything I could do in my business. It included every social media platform I use, in addition to a couple of others that seemed to be the newest craze, my newsletter, my product line, organising photoshoots, brand deals, public speaking and workshop events, writing scripts and filming videos for YouTube, and a whole bunch of other things. The list was about forty items long. It was overwhelming. It got so bad that I eventually experienced "analysis paralysis," where, after spending months trying to do a million things, I became so overwhelmed that I couldn't do anything because I didn't know where to start. I thought everything was important, but, in fact, I was simply busy being busy. I was chasing my tail, trying to do everything, not realising that not everything needed to be done to get the best results and inch myself closer to my goals.

It's understandable to find ourselves in these situations from time to time but it isn't a good idea to stay in this place for long. Setting apart those who live in this constant state of reaction from the people consciously choosing to operate from a place of intention is the presence of an effective work schedule that aligns with one's priorities. Most of us are living as though we have an infinite amount of time to accomplish all the things we'd like. We're all given the

exact same amount of time each day, but how wisely we use
it is what influences the degree to which we live a fulfilling,
happy and successful life. We need to be investing our time in
what matters most to us and stop spending it carelessly or letting
others waste what is our most precious commodity on seemingly
unimportant tasks that are wrapped up in a bow of urgency.

"Lost time is never found again."

–Benjamin Franklin

What I want to emphasise here is that time is precious, so we need
to be more selective with how we spend it, like the way in which you
budget your finances and are selective with how you spend your
hard-earned money. Perhaps this is also why we say things like "I
love *spending time* with you," "You can *save some time,*" "I need to
invest more time," or "I need to better *budget my time.*" In fact, time is
our most precious commodity (after health, of course) because once
we use it, we can't get it back. We can't make more time the way that
we can make more money.

When you account for every moment of your workday and allocate
each minute of the day to a specific job, you begin to live with greater
intention. This shields you from any competing and so-called "priorities"
or distractions. The more you optimise your day, the more you set
yourself up for increased productivity and higher quality work. In doing
so, you also begin to value, respect, and protect your precious time.

Your work schedule, however, isn't designed to be rigid. It's not
meant to hold you to the same timetable each day and week. It
most certainly doesn't have to resemble your now-outdated school
timetable or university calendar. Rather, it's there to act as a

framework to support you, reduce overwhelm, and create space for what's most important to you (your top priorities), all while remaining flexible, moulding to your ever-changing responsibilities, workload, and needs.

To give you an insight into my constantly evolving work schedule, I choose to plan out my days differently, depending on several factors. I spent my late twenties learning a lot about female hormonal health and how our infradian rhythm (a woman's natural twenty-eight-day cycle) and its changes to our levels of estrogen and progesterone influence our overall mood, energy, concentration, desire for social engagement, and level of creativity. After discovering the work of Alisa Vitti, author of *In the Flo*, I became fascinated with syncing my work schedule to my monthly cycle, harnessing the power of my body and working with my natural rhythm and flow. Before I explain further, for those of you not familiar with the different phases of the monthly cycle or wanting a little refresher, I thought I'd briefly recap the four stages: **menstrual, follicular, ovulatory, and luteal**. The menstrual phase lasts around three to seven days and is when hormones, including estrogen and progesterone, are at their lowest. This is an ideal time for rest, reflection, and introspection. It's important to relax, be kind to yourself, evaluate how the previous month has been, and identify any changes needed to create a better upcoming month. The follicular phase lasts around seven to ten days and sees an increase in both estrogen and follicle-stimulating hormone (FSH) in preparation for the maturity and release of an egg. The rise in these hormones and one's energy makes it an ideal time for initiating, preparing, and planning, being creative, dreaming big, and starting new projects. The ovulatory phase follows for a duration of three to four days and sees a dramatic rise in estrogen, followed by a rise in a luteinizing hormone to stimulate the release of an egg. There is also a sharp surge followed by a rapid decline in testosterone. This phase of the cycle brings the natural desire to be more social, communicative, and collaborative. Lastly, we have the luteal phase, which lasts for approximately ten to fourteen days and where, after estrogen, progesterone, and testosterone peak, they fall to their lowest levels right before the menstrual phase of the next cycle begins. This is the "get sh** done" part of the cycle and is great for tying up loose ends and finishing projects.

Okay, so here's how I use this newfound knowledge to influence my schedule: For the past two years, I've committed to taking time off from work during my menstrual phase to honour this part of my cycle and reflect on the month that's been. I consider what went well, what didn't, where I may have overextended myself, and how I can support myself better for the month ahead. I noticed that tasks requiring greater levels of creative energy are naturally easier to focus on during my follicular phase, which is when I like to schedule time to work on new scripts for videos, brainstorm how I will set out the next chapter of my book, and even plan out the next few weeks in my work calendar. On the other hand, networking, socialising, collaboration, and communicating comes most naturally during the ovulatory phase, which is when I now schedule important meetings, along with any film sessions for YouTube. I also tend to schedule most of my social commitments with friends and family around this time of the month. I initially wondered how much of a role my cycle played in my behaviours and natural rhythm. While I've gotten into the habit of structuring my days according to which phase of my cycle I'm experiencing, I believe certain things come more easily to me at different stages of my cycle. For example, and I kid you not, I have this habit of being super productive and either cleaning the entire house, decluttering my closet, cooking and freezing meals to stock up the freezer for weeks in advance, or smashing out a chapter for my

book on the final day of my cycle. It's like my body is telling me to get things done now, with the awareness that I am soon going to need to slow down and take a few days off and enter "sloth mode."

I understand that tailoring your work schedule to this degree to your monthly cycle (if you have one) may not always be possible, depending on the type of work you do. You might, however, still like to learn more about the many ways to honour your monthly cycle through intentional changes and fine-tuning your diet, exercise, social engagements, and work schedule where possible.

Along with trying my best to adapt my work schedule each week to my monthly cycle, I also allow it to be influenced by the amount of work and mental energy I used during the previous month. I typically try to organise my schedule so that a demanding month is followed by a less intense and mentally taxing one, whether that involves scheduling more time for self-care, fewer projects, or more time for fitness.

Lastly, while this isn't always possible, since my work involves assessing and taking on projects that often come out of the blue, it's my preference to reduce my work hours altogether during the summer so that I can enjoy a much-needed break and the all-too-fleeting warmer Melbourne days.

> **"Plan your work for today and every day, then work your plan."**
>
> **–Margaret Thatcher**

Ultimately, what you'll begin to find when you create your
optimised work schedule in this coming chapter, is that it
will help to keep you on track and hold you accountable. A
schedule will help you to decipher what to do, when to do it,
and for how long. Along with your morning routine, it serves as
the backbone for productivity and high-quality work throughout
the day, all while shielding you from time wasters and ensuring you
no longer feel overwhelmed or stressed. Finally, you can rest assured
that the most important tasks will get done without the interruption of
other tasks that otherwise compete for your attention.

Time-Blocking Approach

I started using a time-blocking method back when I was in university.
I didn't realise that I was using a recommended and well-known
method for optimal productivity. At the time, I simply took inspiration
from my high school timetable, where typically we had three to four
subjects a day, each scheduled for either a forty-five- or ninety-minute
block. I figured it would be easier to block out a set amount of time in
my diary each day for working on my assignments and revising for
upcoming exams, like making "mini work appointments" for myself.
As a result, I would often allocate time to focus on one or two units
of my university degree each day and I would strategically schedule
most of my lectures and tutorials for the mornings, leaving me plenty
of time in the afternoon to get my work done. My friends always knew
where to find me. There I was, hiding away upstairs in the library,
sitting with my heavy-as-a-brick textbooks, diary, laptop, notebook,
and, of course, a packet of highlighters laid out in front of me. I
intended to treat my university degree like a nine-to-five job, leaving
my work hat behind as I'd walk out the sliding glass doors of the

library and make my way towards my car, carrying the satisfaction of another day well spent.

While you don't have to adopt a nine-to-five schedule like I did, and I acknowledge that sometimes this isn't possible, I invite you to try out the time-blocking approach, even for a portion of your day. Some people time block their entire day, from waking to sleep; however, I think it's important to leave room for free time and flexibility. The reason I am such a fan of this scheduling method, however, is that it accounts for every single minute and can be a great tool for overcoming procrastination. It helps you to intentionally spend your time by encouraging you to think about what tasks need to get done and when you will commit to seeing them through. This can also be a great productivity tool for anyone who easily gets overwhelmed, much like myself, and has those sporadic "how am I going to get it all done?" freak-outs. I have a lot of different tasks, personal commitments, and responsibilities that need to get done each week, and every time I find myself feeling overwhelmed, I immediately stop and set aside some time to plan out my coming week using the time-blocking method. This is also how I've gone about writing my book. I knew I needed to submit my final manuscript by the middle of this year, so I worked backwards, scheduling into my diary numerous four-hour blocks of writing over the span of ten months. I knew that simply writing in my diary "work on chapter x" on any given day wasn't going to do it for me. When would I sit down at my desk? For how long? What about those other commitments that have earned an actual time stamp in my diary like "drop off Winston to doggy day-care at 8:00 a.m." or "meeting with my videographer at 2:00 p.m."? Then there are those unaccounted-for temptations like TV, social media, chatting to friends over the phone or catching up in person. Surely, they'd take precedence, and the book writing will simply have to wait for another day. This is exactly why we need the time-blocking approach: so that everything important to us rightfully gets our attention and we enter each day with a plan of attack.

The way that the time-blocking approach works is quite simple. You write down the hours of the day, what you aim to focus on, and when, ideally working in thirty- to sixty-minute blocks to avoid jumping from task to task. You can even go one step further and colour-code tasks or subjects (e.g., emails = orange, meetings = blue, etc.). Ideally, you'll want to block out a significant portion of your schedule for more demanding tasks to give yourself enough time to make some good progress without hopping to the next task. Of course, if you are blocking out, say, four hours to work on your book, you still need to make sure you take regular breaks. I personally try to get up and get moving every thirty to forty-five minutes; however, the Pomodoro technique is a great strategy to help you maintain focus and energy. Simply set a timer for twenty-five minutes and each time it goes off, take five minutes to get up and get moving.

Another thing to keep in mind when creating your work schedule is to make sure you display it somewhere you will regularly see. Having your schedule displayed is nonnegotiable. You can write it out in a bullet journal, schedule it in a digital calendar, or like me, design a weekly work timetable online and save it as a JPEG file to display as the wallpaper for your laptop and desktop computer.

Here's a snippet from my current weekly work schedule:

Monday

9:00 a.m.	Head to the office
9:30 a.m.	Deep Work
10:00 a.m.	Deep Work
10:30 a.m.	Deep Work
11:00 a.m.	Deep Work
11:30 a.m.	Deep Work
12:00 p.m.	Deep Work
12:30 p.m.	Deep Work
1:00 p.m.	Lunch
1:30 p.m.	Lunch
2:00 p.m.	Post on socials
2:30 p.m.	Reply to emails
3:00 p.m.	Pack up/Home time

I designed my schedule so that when I see it displayed on my laptop, I see that "Deep Work" is colour-coded in blue, "Post on socials" in pink, and "Reply to emails" in yellow to give me a visual representation of how I plan to spend my day in the office.

Given my constantly changing work commitments, I decided to use the term "Deep Work" rather than specify the exact task. This is something I note down in my diary instead. Also, any to-dos that are not already accounted for get scheduled towards the end of my workday once I have spent a significant portion of my morning allocated to getting my best work done. I will make time for personal to-dos outside of work hours.

A note on chronotypes:

Remember that we all have a natural inclination regarding the times of day when we prefer to work, sleep, or feel most alert or energetic. I'm naturally most alert between the hours of 9:00 a.m. to 3:00 p.m., which is when I get my best work done. I understand that not everyone is a morning person and so you may choose to schedule your "deep work" for later in the morning or even into the evening when the house is quiet or the library is empty, and you feel calm and alert and can get some solid work done. To be clear, I still stand by the importance of scheduling top priorities before other tasks. Whenever you sit down to work, your level of focus, attention, and energy is at its greatest for that session. Don't waste it on unimportant tasks that could otherwise wait and don't need the same level of mental energy.

Productivity Pro Tip:

Write down the *task* you plan to work on rather than what you aim to complete. Setting a firm completion goal can result in rising stress levels as you work against the clock to finish the task in time. Instead, allow yourself plenty of time with respect to upcoming deadlines and say to yourself, "During this time, I plan to work on the following task."

A note on priorities:

It's no surprise that most books I read tend to be about productivity and self-development. A few years ago, I was reading up on the concept or growing movement of Essentialism—the idea that we can achieve more through doing less when we focus our attention on our top priority and become more intentional with what we give our attention and energy to. While researching, I was surprised to learn that the term "priority" used to be used as a singular term and rarely would people talk about multiple priorities. That's because, contrary to many people's beliefs in today's day and age of overstimulation that embodies the glorification of being busy, not everything can be a priority. Nor *should* everything be a priority. What's most important to you will depend on your long-term goals and values. I remember once lying down in a yoga class and listening to the teacher recite a few short poems. One of the passages resonated with me and while I never managed to stumble across it again, the message remains with me. It went something along the lines of:

Every day, the world takes you by the hand and tries to pull you in many directions, whispering this is important, this is urgent, and this too. It's then up to us to say, no, this is important, and decide how we will spend our time and energy.

You'll have noticed that I scheduled my workdays to begin with deep work. This is when I prioritise my most mentally demanding tasks that require more focus and attention than others and often make up my top priority for the day. Inspired by the work of Cal Newport, author of *Deep Work*, I only ever allocate up to four hours of deep work each day, as this is where my threshold lies before I can start to feel drained, and the quality of my work can suffer. Deep work involves working on tasks that require a high level of mental energy and concentration. It's best scheduled for when you are feeling most alert, energised, and fresh, as this sort of work is particularly demanding. For me, deep work can involve writing scripts, working on my book, or working on other major projects I've secured. If you're yet to familiarise yourself with his work, he also highlights the importance of scheduling "shallow" work or tasks that require less mental energy and concentration for later in the day. As you can see, some of my shallow tasks include checking and replying to emails and posting on social media (e.g., I schedule a separate time to thoughtfully plan and write my Instagram captions, which falls under deep work). They can also involve other tasks such as making appointments or designing YouTube video thumbnails. All these tasks hitch a ride on the tail end of my workday when I have less mental energy to give. Also, if I didn't manage to complete my shallow tasks for the day, it's unlikely there would be any long-term negative implications for my career. Just as prioritising the wrong kind of tasks in the morning can be a source of noise and negativity that zaps your mental clarity (namely scrolling online or consuming the news), so too can prioritising the wrong kind of tasks as part of your work schedule, especially if they happen to be someone else's priority and not your own. While I prefer to focus on one main work priority for the day, I understand this may not be possible for everyone. As I briefly mentioned earlier, when I was a university student, I would block out time each day for consolidating class notes, working on assignments, and exam revision. The trick was to allow enough time for myself to become immersed in a task and make good progress before moving on to the next task. For me, this is at least forty-five minutes. Perhaps your deep work involves working on a presentation for forty-five minutes, followed by sixty minutes for researching and reading relevant articles, and then another forty-five minutes of note-taking and summarising information.

A note on to-do lists:

While we're on the topic of priorities and scheduling, I thought I'd mention that I used to be a huge fan of creating to-do lists. The act of working my way through a long list and checking it off gave me a sense of accomplishment; however, I soon learned that to-do lists were a major source of stress and overwhelm, and they diminished my overall level of productivity. Sure, I was motivated to get as many of my tasks done as soon as possible to earn my next hit of dopamine (mixed with a cocktail of relief), but it came at the cost of being able to do some of my best work. I would begin my day by "eating the frog," getting all my to-dos done first thing, which used my precious and limited energy that could have otherwise been better spent on working on my top priorities and high mental energy tasks. They would often take longer than expected. Then I tried allocating a set time in my work schedule to batch my to-dos and complete them towards the end of the day if they weren't time-sensitive. This seemed to work much better for me and remains my recommended approach for ensuring your smaller tasks and to-dos still get the attention they deserve without being at the expense of your top priorities.

Here's an example of a recent to-do list:

* Email my editor re: this week's YouTube video upload

* Send invoice for brand deal

* Schedule Winston's fur cut

* Order new driver's license to be delivered to updated address

* Post on Instagram stories

* Buy new satchels for sending out stationery orders

❋   Pack and send out Educationery order from last night

Not every day has this many tasks; however, as you can probably see, if I'd start my day with this list, I'd use up quite a lot of my initial tank of energy on seemingly unimportant tasks.

Setting Time Limits

Whether you're a workaholic—I mean, enthusiastic worker—or lack the motivation to get your work done, it's important to set clear time limits when designing your work schedule. This works well for several reasons. If you're prone to overdoing it, having clear work boundaries will help prevent brain fog, fatigue, and burnout. If you lack motivation, it also helps you to practise self-discipline and keeps you accountable for meeting each of the work appointments you've made with yourself. Knowing that you only have a finite amount of time to get your work done also signals to yourself that while you may not be looking forward to completing the tasks that await you, the workday will soon be coming to an end, and you can look forward to some well-deserved time off.

Whether working from home or in the office, I always do my best to stick to my schedule. It can be tempting to work later into the evening when working from home because my work and personal environments tend to blur into one; however, my work schedule is there to remind me that I have planned out my day thoughtfully for optimal productivity and that straying too far from this schedule isn't always a good idea. If you happen to work from home or have the liberty of choosing how you structure your days entirely, then your schedule can be a source of stability and much-needed structure. On the other hand, an optimal work schedule that helps you create space to focus on your top priorities, decide when to respond to emails and identify whether you're in the position to take on others' requests can be your antidote to the many competing tasks that come with working in an office environment. This is especially the case where much of your day might be made up of meetings and replying to emails, all while juggling your own tasks in between.

> **"Don't wait for the motivation to start. Start and the motivation will come."**
>
> **–Anonymous**

An Activity to Spark Action:

Use the time-blocking method in the spaces that follow to create your optimal work routine. Remember to schedule all your responsibilities and tasks for the day. Feel free to add your morning routine at the start and even colour-code your tasks to better represent your overall day.

* Remember, writing down how you plan to spend your time will help you stick to this new work schedule.

	Monday	**Tuesday**
7:00 a.m.		
7:30 a.m.		
8:00 a.m.		
8:30 a.m.		
9:00 a.m.		

9:30 a.m.		
10:00 a.m.		
10:30 a.m.		
11:00 a.m.		
11:30 a.m.		
12:00 p.m.		
12:30 p.m.		
1:00 p.m.		
1:30 p.m.		
2:00 p.m.		
2:30 p.m.		
3:00 p.m.		
3:30 p.m.		
4:00 p.m.		
4:30 p.m.		
5:00 p.m.		
5:30 p.m.		

	Wednesday	**Thursday**
7:00 a.m.		
7:30 a.m.		
8:00 a.m.		
8:30 a.m.		
9:00 a.m.		
9:30 a.m.		
10:00 a.m.		
10:30 a.m.		
11:00 a.m.		
11:30 a.m.		
12:00 p.m.		
12:30 p.m.		
1:00 p.m.		
1:30 p.m.		
2:00 p.m.		
2:30 p.m.		

3:00 p.m.		
3:30 p.m.		
4:00 p.m.		
4:30 p.m.		
5:00 p.m.		
5:30 p.m.		

	Friday
7:00 a.m.	
7:30 a.m.	
8:00 a.m.	
8:30 a.m.	
9:00 a.m.	
9:30 a.m.	
10:00 a.m.	
10:30 a.m.	
11:00 a.m.	

11:30 a.m.	
12:00 p.m.	
12:30 p.m.	
1:00 p.m.	
1:30 p.m.	
2:00 p.m.	
2:30 p.m.	
3:00 p.m.	
3:30 p.m.	
4:00 p.m.	
4:30 p.m.	
5:00 p.m.	
5:30 p.m.	

Whichever way you choose to design your work schedule, I invite you to implement the following five work habits to support your overall productivity throughout the day:

* Schedule your top priorities earlier in the day.

* Batch your to-dos and allocate time for them in your schedule, following your top priority.

  * Allow yourself enough time on each item to enable you to make good progress and immerse yourself in the task at hand.

  * Use the time-blocking method to account for all your time in the day (lunch and tea breaks included).

* Take a short five- to ten-minute break to get moving and refocus every thirty to forty minutes.

PART 2:

Finding your Flow

CHAPTER 3:

Getting into the Work Zone

**"Mastering others is strength;
mastering yourself is true power."**

–Lao Tzu

My intention for this next section is to help you maximise your
overall level of productivity when working so that you can get your
work done with a greater level of ease and carve out more space
for yourself each day. We're going for a "work hard, plan hard"
mentality here. When you're working, you are laser-focused and
committed to getting your tasks done successfully. When you're
outside of work hours and resting, you're fully committed to using
this time intentionally and recharging your energy. Remember that
you cannot be in a constant state of productivity. Like nature, nothing
blooms all year round.

I've come across a lot of work-life balance books that advocate
prioritising more time for self-care. They talk about the harmful
implications of glorifying busyness. They shine a light on the
masculine-dominated way of living and how the demand for constant
productivity and output is taking a physical and mental toll on all of

us. The problem is, they fail to help people successfully carve out more time in the week, let alone day, for much-needed rest. They are based on the premise that if something's truly important to you, you'll make time for it. True. I agree that when something or someone is important, people have a way of making time in their day, but it doesn't address how they are spending their time at work and whether that person's work life or approach to work could use some assistance.

A few years back, I posted an Instagram graphic with five things to do each day for self-care. While a lot of the feedback was positive, some of the more mature people who follow my Instagram account left responses like, "I simply don't have enough time." Or "Try working full time and being a mum while prioritising all five of these things!" At first, I took these negative responses they'd left underneath my pink Instagram graphic to heart. Then I realised they were constructive pieces of feedback and that each person had a good point. How can I expect my community to prioritise meditation, exercise, journaling, getting outside, or having a creative hobby, if I don't also help them *make* time for themselves each day?

A large part of my work is around maximising one's productivity and improving time-management skills; however, the other focus I regularly take is on self-care, mental health, and wellbeing. I'm passionate about both, which means I'm passionate about work-life balance. My passion is further fuelled by the hundreds of requests I receive every year for more productivity and stress management tips that continue to guide my work.

To have sufficient time off to relax and recharge, you need to ensure that you are your most efficient and productive self when you sit down to work. Things like having a good work routine and

structure, or getting clear on your priorities, as we've previously
discussed, will absolutely help you get your work done, but
we also need to address other obstacles to productivity such
as distractions, technology timewasters, and the procrastination
bug, all of which can lead to increased anxiety and stress
if unaddressed.

Before I get into the best ways for maximising your productivity,
I wanted to first touch on an important concept that also sparked
inspiration for this book. The concept I'm referring to is known as
"flow," but you might know it as "work zone" or "study zone." They
all refer to or reflect this state of deep productivity and progress
and the feeling of satisfaction that comes with it. This is what you're
striving for, being your most productive self. When I think about the
word "flow," I associate it with feelings of ease, relaxation, and
success. We're moving with the waves rather than pushing against
them and getting knocked down. I've found that the best way to live
life is to "go with the flow" and do my best to release any resistance
I put up along the way. When I approach life in this way, everything
seems to work out. Maybe you've also found this to be true?

Back when I was brainstorming title options for this book with a
few friends, we workshopped the idea of "Finding Your Flow."
We decided against using the word "flow" by itself because
a few of them instantly jumped to thinking about a woman's
monthly cycle. Given that I didn't want my readers to get the
wrong idea about the content in this book, we went back to the
drawing board. If I think about it, though, in this context, the term
"flow" was chosen to refer to the menstrual cycle of a woman, not
because it was used in the literal sense, but because it reflects the
idea that a woman is in fact in sync with the natural cycle, rhythm,
and flow of Mother Earth. Some women still refer to it as their

moon cycle because many found that their bodies would sync with the cycle of the full moon.

Perhaps you've heard the term "flow" used more recently with respect to one's level of productivity. I filmed a YouTube video a while ago on this topic and after researching about it, I learned how this term came about and what it means. The term "flow" was coined by Hungarian American psychologist Mihaly Csikszentmihalyi. In his words, flow is "a state in which people are so involved in an activity that nothing else seems to matter." To further unpack this term, it's when your mind isn't wandering and thinking about what you need to be doing next, who you need to call, or how you can't believe you mixed up your 8:00 a.m. meeting this morning with your editor in The States and got the time zone wrong. (Whoops!) Instead, you are involved in what you are doing right now. You don't hear the cars on the street. You don't notice whether your dog is sleeping on the armchair in front of you or in his bed next to your feet. You are too immersed in what you're doing to notice any of those things. Take a moment to reflect on a time when you have been completely immersed in a task. A time when you've been so focused on what you're doing that you become oblivious to the outside world. I experience this a lot whenever I write. I get so consumed by my ideas and how to communicate them through my writing that I am always surprised to see the clock move forward in two-hour increments. I don't just experience this with writing. It can be filming videos, attending a dance class, and even painting. One winter afternoon Adam went out with his friends and I stayed home, painting with watercolours and decorating my art by arranging and gluing dried flowers. Four hours later, my tea light candles were just about to finish burning and I realised I needed to make myself some dinner since it was approaching 9:00 p.m.! If you can relate to these instances, it's likely you have also experienced this state of flow. Flow is one of the most enjoyable states of being because we are wrapped in the present moment and can be more creative, productive, and happy. When we enter a state of flow, we arrive at the much-sought-after place of least resistance and the greatest level of momentum. This is where our focus and attention are at their all-time highest as we immerse ourselves in a task. We feel most at ease and time can seem to fly by. It's where your mind goes when you sit down to work and upon finally looking at the clock, you find that you have lost yourself for some time in the task. Nothing and no one had interrupted you and your mind was laser-focused on one thing.

If this is where we get our best work done, why do so many people often find it hard to successfully get into a state of flow? In today's environment, there is an ever-increasing number of distractions and temptations that try, and often successfully manage, to pull us away from a place of deep productivity. Social media, technology, open-plan offices, at-home distractions, and competing priorities are all some of the many obstacles we experience on any given day or even hour. When it comes to staying in flow, there's also a catch. Once you enter this state, should something or someone pull your attention away from the task and break your focus, it can take considerable time and discipline to make your way back to this place of momentum and optimal productivity.

Having an optimal work schedule is the first step to getting into the work/study zone or finding flow; however, we can't snap our fingers and immediately find ourselves in this place. We need to give it time. Of course, there are ways of reducing the amount of time it can take to reach this state of flow (which I will share more about in the coming chapters); however, most people sabotage themselves by being impulsive and succumbing to temptations (a.k.a., distractions) because they lack the self-discipline required to avoid picking up their phones or turning to the person next to them for a quick chat. For those who do manage to steer clear of procrastination and temptation, too many end up choosing to walk out of the gates of productivity, too often for the most trivial of reasons (usually to check their phone halfway through) and then wonder why they got locked out upon trying to instantly re-enter. We are so used to living in a state of constant stimulation, of "doing" and "consuming," that our minds have become conditioned to hop from one thing to the next rather than stay on task. But this is exactly what we *need* to be doing if we want to *actually* get our work done and with ease. No wonder it's such a sought-after state. If only it were that easy to enter whenever you wanted. Or is it?

Rather than trying to force it, I'm going to share with you how to enter this state to significantly increase your overall level of productivity and quality of work, minimise procrastination, overcome barriers to motivation, and improve your focus and concentration. Beginning your work routine from this state of flow isn't a passive approach. It requires you to change your habits, tune into your body, and hold yourself accountable. In the chapters that follow, I will share what has helped me reach this destination day after day to get my best work done. We'll explore several simple yet powerful ways to enter this state before addressing how to navigate and overcome the many obstacles to flow, so that you can remain in this place of greatest momentum for longer lengths of time. I'll also share my effective strategies to help you get back on track and more easily re-enter this state of momentum.

CHAPTER 4:

Creating a Productive Work Environment

"I've got a theory: if you love your workspace, you'll love your work a little more."

–Cynthia Rowley

Our physical environment plays a significant role in helping us more easily enter and remain in a state of deep productivity. You might have already noticed how your work environment can impact your focus, concentration, and mood. Luckily, the significant influence of this element, most of the time, is well within our control. It's simply a matter of identifying the different aspects that affect our overall productivity and motivation because, without awareness, we cannot implement the necessary changes. Regardless of whether you are working from home, in the school library, in a hotel while travelling for work, or in the office, several key elements make a work environment favourable to getting into a state of flow.

For your environment to help effortlessly prime you into a state of deep productivity, it needs to meet a few criteria. Before I elaborate on this, know that your workspace doesn't have to look like something out of Pinterest, but it does need to be clutter-free, calming, project professionalism, and meet your noise needs. I'll preface by saying that while I'm not a minimalist, I try to keep my home—and, importantly, my workspace—clutter-free. I like to keep only the necessary items on display, along with a couple of house plants, candles, and currently, a lovely potted white orchid that my best friend gave me for my birthday earlier this year (which I've managed to successfully care for).

I take most of my video meetings and interviews from my home office, where I get the best natural light and have all my audio and camera gear already set up. Just the other month, I was being interviewed about my work on a video call when I was asked whether I practise minimalism on account of having such a tidy office! Bear in mind that the backdrop of my video calls includes Adam's desk, which he often packs up before heading into the office a couple of days a week, so there isn't too much to look at on camera. He's also a passionate Aussie football fan and the artwork he decided to display above his desk is our team's mascot in cartoon illustration form. The whole family barracks for the Melbourne Football Club, whose mascot is…a devil. When they won the premiership in 2021, they released a special poster featuring their beloved mascot, along with fire, a trident and an animated pair of eyes *beaming* back at you. The little guy isn't quite on brand, so unfortunately for him, he doesn't get invited to attend my video calls and instead takes a temporary seat on the floor, leaving the white wall blank.

If you're interested in seeing my home office setup, I have filmed quite a few "updated office tour" videos on my YouTube channel, *Study With Jess*, over the years.

If you have a desk at home or in the office, spend an afternoon looking at what is displayed that gets used regularly and could be considered an essential, compared to anything taking up unnecessary space and causing clutter. Do you have multiple photo frames of family or other sentimentals taking up space on your desk that might be better suited to the bedroom? Are there piles of books, notes, notebooks, or receipts lying around? Do you have handfuls of pens and other stationery when you only need a couple at arm's length? One of the benefits of a coworking space is that hot desking requires you to only keep the essentials on you and it never gives you the opportunity to invite clutter into a work session. I pack my laptop, charger, notepad, a pen, and glasses in my bag the night before and nothing else makes the cut.

More recently, when Adam and I found ourselves working from home for the majority of 2021 when our state experienced several extended lockdowns during the pandemic, I often opted to work from the dining table. A lot of his work consists of phone calls and meetings, and I found the noise distracting, so instead, working from the dining room gave me the space and peace I needed to concentrate. Despite having a table that seats up to twelve people, I felt agitated and craved more space, so I decided to declutter the dining table too. I refrained from using it as a place to leave unopened mail and packages or recently worn sweaters, moved our candlesticks to the fireplace mantle, the fruit bowl to the shelving unit, and would often keep the table bare, almost as if to create a blank canvas for me to prop up my laptop and create my work.

You can also apply this approach anywhere you may find yourself working. I even used it when I travelled from Sydney to Los Angeles for a job with Netflix a few years ago and decided to spend a few hours writing while thirty-thousand feet in the air. I remember having

quite heightened anxiety that morning about getting on the flight and felt homesick because I was waiting for one more month to pass until Adam and I finally moved back home to Melbourne after living in Sydney for a little over a year. Work has always been an effective distraction, so I decided to use it as an opportunity to focus on something else and ease my mind. The tiny tray tables certainly don't compare to a functioning desk or dining table, but I managed to make do. I don't know about you, but I get flustered when I'm in a small space and have a lot of things lying around. Magazines, my carry-on luggage, a drink, snacks, noise-cancelling headphones, my travel pillow, and jacket were all taking up unnecessary real estate and stressing me out. Once I put everything away so that only my laptop and a cup of chamomile tea that the air hostess had brought over for me were on my tray table, I could finally get some work done. From memory, I spent over three hours writing more than a few thousand words on that flight.

I am most certainly a creature of comfort—I am a Cancerian, after all—and one thing I've learned over the years since starting my business and working from home and in an office space is that our environment can be used to influence our productivity by way of altering our mood. A calming environment evokes feelings of ease and helps us feel centred and more relaxed, which in turn helps our overall level of focus and concentration. If we consider the stress x productivity relationship, we know that too much stress inhibits our ability to concentrate, exercise good judgement, and produce our best quality work. With our work environments changing regularly, you may not be able to rely solely on working from the comfort of your at-home setup, that incorporates natural essential oils, candles, your vision board for inspiration and a fresh bunch of flowers or your rapidly multiplying house plants. The trick is to find ways of inviting

more calm into wherever you choose to work, whether that's
opting for a cosy café where the smell of a fresh chai latte or
long black encourages you to inhale deeply and sit back into
your comfy armchair, or coworking space that's full of indoor
plants to enliven its members. You might even like to bring some
calm into your space by spraying your own invigorating room
mist, making herbal tea, or popping on a pair of noise-cancelling
headphones and listening to a cosy jazz playlist.

On that note, I also want to encourage you to think about your
optimal noise levels and work ambience. This will be different for
everyone. I invite you to try out three different noise levels to discover
which one works best for you. These are music, chatter, and silence.
Personally, I get my best work done either in silence or when playing
background music through my headphones. Chatter doesn't do
it for me, which is probably why I always chose to study in silent
rooms at school, at the local library, or in my little study cave (a.k.a.,
my bedroom). Try playing music like bossa nova, lo-fi beats, or
background jazz to see whether this helps maintain your focus. If you
seek chatter, work from a café, coworking space, the non-silent area
of a library, or listen to a background chatter playlist when trying to
get some deep work done. If you need silence, opt for a quiet room
at home or in the library, or wear noise-cancelling headphones to
drown out unwanted distractions and voices.

I've also found that I can more easily enter a state of deep
productivity or flow when I feel inspired and my environment projects
professionalism. There's been a huge increase in the need for home
offices recently, as people began to see the benefits of being in the
office part-time and working from home (WFH) several days a week.
This increase in the demand for more space also saw an increase in
brands sharing more professional WFH inspiration, organisation,

and ideas. Creating a professional WFH setup with the right lighting, quality camera and audio equipment, and furniture designed to meet your ergonomic needs and avoid headaches and a tight neck all became topics of conversation, and for a good reason.

In addition to these common elements, I began taking a deeper interest in how our environment, and more specifically, in this case, our workspace, plays a role in our success. I took it upon myself and began researching the art of Feng Shui. If you are not yet familiar with Feng Shui, it is an ancient Chinese traditional practice based upon a system of laws considered to govern spatial arrangement and orientation in relation to the flow of energy (chi). The belief underlying this practice is that we can change the energy forces around us by changing the orientation of objects and introducing or subtracting different materials such as metal or wood to harmonise individuals with their surrounding environment. I spent hours watching webinars, listening to podcasts, and reading blogs to better understand the small but powerful changes I could make to my home office. What I learned was fascinating, and while it was all new to me, the principles make complete sense, so I optimistically invite you to apply them to your daily life.

Let's begin with your desk—the place where all the magic happens. Your desk should be made of a sturdy and durable material like wood because other material such as a glass desktop can shatter. The reasoning behind this is that you want to ensure that the foundation upon which you work will be as strong as possible.

The size of your desk is also important to consider. A desk that is too small can result in clutter and not creating enough space to welcome new opportunities. A desk too large, on the other hand, can lead you to feel overwhelmed, as though you have taken on too much.

Next, your desk's positioning and where you sit in the room, also referred to as "The Power Position." The Power Position requires you to be sitting down and facing the doorway to symbolically be open to new opportunities. Interestingly, I was speaking to my videographer, James, who shared that he recently changed the orientation of his desk since moving to a new office. He'd noticed that since moving his desk so that he was now facing the doorway, more people would come into his office to say hi. Perhaps the change in his body language was more inviting since he no longer had his back to the door, or maybe energetically, he was also open to more networking and collaboration.

Another piece of inspiration I took from my research about Feng Shui principles was to create a "Success Wall." When we moved into our home, we installed two white floating shelves next to our desks. Displayed on my shelf are copies of my books, my 100k subscriber plaque from YouTube, the study planners I designed for Educationery, and a clear quartz crystal. A success wall can include your trophies, medals, a framed cut-out of an article you wrote that was featured in the paper, books from your favourite authors who embody success, elements of gold or silver—two colours that reflect abundance, or anything else that symbolises success to you. The intention is to bring inspiration to your space and remind yourself of your achievements and desires because where attention goes, energy flows. When you focus on success, you attract more of it.

I like to apply these success principles of Feng Shui outside the home. It can be as simple as opting to work at a desk that faces a doorway rather than having your back to everyone. You could even create a digital vision board and save it to your laptop's home screen for added inspiration. In Melbourne, we have a beautiful and old library in the city called the State Library. Its grand high ceilings, floor-to-ceiling bookshelves, old wooden desks and table lamps, polished hardwood floors, and leather upholstered couches make it one of the most enchantingly inviting places to work. I spent most of my final high school year studying with friends in the State Library for this reason. Sometimes, surrounding yourself with an environment that exudes success and productivity is what you need to find your flow.

Questions to help you identify your ideal working environment:

* Are there particular places where you feel most productive?
  If so, write them down here:

_____

_____

_____

_____

_____

* What time of day do you notice you are more productive and feel in flow?

_____

_____

_____

_____

_____

✳ Is there a particular time of day when you feel less productive
   or out of flow?

_____

_____

_____

_____

_____

✳ When you're most productive, do you need quiet, background
   chatter, or music?

_____

_____

_____

_____

_____

Consider how you might like to incorporate the tips I've covered
throughout this chapter into your work routine and environment.

It might be time to change your work environment, try out some new settings, and find out what works best for you. Remember, we aren't striving for a perfect work environment in the sense that it requires a $1,000 spending spree at IKEA. Often, it takes a good decluttering, a little reorganising, making sure you've invested in the right equipment for you to get your work done, and a comfortable desk and chair setup. Pair that with the right ambience for your working style and you're good to go!

CHAPTER 5:

Starting Rituals

"Rituals cut through and operate on everything besides the 'head' level."

–Aiden Kelly

If you love a good motivational quote as much as I do, then you might have already come across the quote, "Don't wait for the motivation to start. Start and the motivation will come." I've found there's a lot of truth to these words of wisdom. When I commit to sticking to my work schedule and the different tasks I've incorporated into my day's plan, I find that even on those days when I don't feel in the mood to work, let alone write several thousand words, somehow, I always find myself in flow and letting go of that initial resistance I was holding onto. Okay, maybe not *somehow*, because I can't credit my productivity to random luck. Truth is, unlike this quote suggests, I don't just sit down, open my laptop, and let out my strong "taskmaster" from her cage that makes up a (sometimes large) part of my personality. Instead, I've found a better way of starting my work sessions that doesn't make me feel as though I am chained to my desk like a student in detention but rather invites a sense of ease and calm into the initial process of starting—which is where we find the greatest level of resistance. Starting my work sessions more mindfully and with intention guides me down the path of productivity and leads to the best results and highest quality work.

There's an oversimplification embedded within this quote because it assumes that the act of starting isn't without obstacles. Yes, a lot of us are waiting for the feeling of motivation to start something, but unless we are working on something we are super passionate about 100 percent of the time (which is rarely the case), we need to equip ourselves with the tools that build momentum and can overcome the initial resistance or friction we feel towards starting. Even when I'm working on a project that I feel passionate about, such as writing a book, working on a web series, or collaborating with a global brand on new content for social media, the truth is that even in these instances, I do not always feel highly motivated every single time I show up to work on them. Then, there are tasks that we don't look forward to doing, regardless of the day of the week, or that evoke a level of stress, overwhelm, or general reluctance. I'll go deeper into the reasons behind procrastination and the antidotes for these in the coming chapters, but for now, I want to emphasise that this idea of "just start" just doesn't work. At least, not in isolation.

For as long as I can remember, I have been starting my work sessions with the help of pre-work rituals, also known as starting rituals. These rituals assist you in gaining momentum and entering a state of flow by priming you into a headspace for productive work. Importantly, once they become a habit, they act as a cue. Ultimately, I want you to turn your work sessions into a more positive experience. If you're experiencing resistance, your starting rituals are there to help you ease into your work sessions and give you something to look forward to. They also act as little doses of self-care before you sit down to work and help to alleviate feelings of stress by stilling your mind. It might sound like a fancy and time-consuming thing to do, but I promise you, this is not the case. Throughout this chapter, I'll share with you a range of different and easy to implement rituals to help you live in your flow, especially when it comes to your work life, where we too often experience stress and procrastination.

How can rituals help you? Rituals can be a beautiful and valuable addition to your work sessions by helping you to create a work routine that works for you. Rituals have particularly been utilised in meditation and spiritual practices for hundreds of years. They have become sacred acts that reconnect humans to a higher power, such as Mother Nature, the Universe, G-d, or to anchor us back to ourselves and reconnect with the most centred, calm, and pure part of who we are. By introducing some simple rituals before you begin your work, you can regain a sense of calm in your days, and increase your overall focus and efficiency. As I shared earlier, when talking about the importance of an optimal morning routine, daily rituals are a great way to prepare your mind and body for what's to come. For example, your morning meditation or workout can be used to prepare you for the day ahead, whereas enjoying a peaceful soak in the bath or reading a few pages of a good book before bed can help prepare you for a good night's sleep. Your starting rituals can therefore be used to prepare you before you're about to sit down and work.

I wanted to share with you some of my favourite rituals to begin my work routine. This is by no means a finite list. Simply let these rituals inspire you and your upcoming work sessions, sparking other ideas for future rituals you might like to incorporate. You'll see that these rituals work to awaken different senses, including smell, sight, touch, and hearing, to take you on a sensory journey and lead you to the destination of deep productivity and flow.

Working with Tea

The key to a beautiful tea ritual is in the details. Allow yourself to indulge in a beautiful tea and brew it from a special teapot or mug that you'll enjoy using while you work. In many countries, such as China or Japan, tea and tea ceremonies are sacred rituals, so it's important to savour the moment. The intention is to slow down. It's an opportunity to be mindful and align oneself with the flow of nature. When you make yourself a tea, use it as an invitation to be present and take in the entire experience. Notice the details, no matter how small. Gaze at the rising steam and feel the heat of the mug as you hold it between your hands. Try to smell the flavours of the tea leaves as they unveil and begin to get acquainted with each other. If you add milk to your tea, you might pour the milk into your mug before letting the milk clouds move through the tea until the ripple of the milk completes its job and everything becomes still once again. No need to stir. No need to rush. Just let it be.

Tea is one of the first rituals I relied on when I was in my early to mid-twenties and working on a telephone crisis helpline. I'd make myself a chamomile tea in the breakroom before each session. I remember taking my tea to my desk, where I would then write down a positive affirmation at the top of my notebook to keep me focused through difficult calls. Even though I didn't know anything about pre-work rituals, I found this sacred pause necessary for preparation. It gave me the time I needed to collect my thoughts for the work I was about to do. As I would cup my hands around the comforting warmth of my mug, each sip of chamomile brought me clarity and calm to remain my centred self and help others through their difficulties.

Not surprisingly, one of the first things I did when Adam and I moved into our home this year was stock up on all our nonperishables for our pantry and set up a tea station. I pride myself on giving my family and friends a long response to "What teas do you have?" each time they visit. If you come to my house and request a particular tea, trust that if I don't have it on the day, it will be there waiting for you next time you visit. I am the "Tea Queen." I should mention that I always try to buy high-quality tea. I try to make sure it's organic, comes in recycled cardboard packaging and biodegradable "plastic," and is also loose-leaf. I also have a few special teas that I like to use as part of my starting rituals. My favourite now is a beau-tea-ful (see what I did there?) blend of peppermint, lemon balm, and lemon verbena that is also tied in first place with my other favourite, a lemongrass and ginger blend. I have a couple of mugs I repeatedly like to use, although this does defeat the purpose of having a mug collection, since I don't seem to be rotating them often! If you watch my videos on YouTube, you might guess which mug is my current favourite to use when working. It's a white mug with a gold handle, a little gold illustration of hands in a prayer position on the inside, and on the outside, it says "gratitude." I've even made a few mugs in pottery class but I always forget that by the time they enter the kiln for firing, they shrink 20–25 percent and so they are now used as mini vases or to store my pottery carving tools.

Working with Scent

Fragrance is another excellent, calming, and sometimes invigorating sensory marker to incorporate and rely on. You might have a scent or fragrance you like to work with, such as incense, room sprays, or candles, all of which can act as sensory markers to set your mind up for productive work. Different smells can be used for

different purposes. You might like to use lavender or lemongrass
to ease feelings of stress, cedarwood to ground and centre you, or
peppermint, eucalyptus, and citrus fragrances to keep you feeling
focused and alert. Before I sit down to work, I love to burn an
essential oil or light a homemade soy candle. Along with tea, my
candle obsession is real and has become internationally known.
A few months ago, I received an email from a teacher in the UK
sharing his students' PowerPoint presentations on productivity
and study skills. I could *not* believe it. I was shocked and
incredibly humbled. The students had chosen to create
their projects based on my YouTube videos! There I was,
in these students' presentation slides. Photos, headshots,
and screenshots of my videos. They had summarised a lot of
my content into dot points, sharing their favourite productivity
and organisational tips, along with fun facts about me. As I read
through each presentation, I came across my all-time favourite slide.
One of the slides read, "I'm Jess and I love CANDLES!" Brilliant.
Pure, innocent, accurate brilliance. This grade-six student decided to
mention my love of candles in their presentation about productivity
because they knew how important it was to me. They included it
because candles are one way that I have created a calming work
environment and signal to my mind that it's time to get some good
work done. That, or they just figured that I must love candles. Either
way, I loved it.

When choosing candles, essential oil blends, or incense, make
sure to choose a scent that resonates with you. Those made from
natural materials are best because you'll be breathing it in. I love to
use Australian-made, natural, handmade, soy-based candles with
organic cotton wicks and opt for ones that use essential oils rather
than synthetic perfumes. Beeswax candles are another wonderful
option. They give a sweet-smelling aroma and are a beautiful and

natural way to cleanse the air. My best friend Lanz bought me
this amazing gold lighter that powers through a USB port so
I don't go through matches anymore. I press a button and it
looks like a little electrical current at the tip that zaps the candle's
wick alight. As I try to describe it, I'm aware that it sounds a lot
like I am mercilessly electrocuting my candles; however, I promise
it's soothing! (Disclaimer: no candles were hurt in the writing of
this book.)

If you choose to incorporate candles into your pre-work ritual, make it
a mindful practice. Notice the sound of the lighter, watch as the wick
catches flame, gently place the candle down, and notice how taking
this precious pause in your day to set yourself up for a productive
work session can ground you. I love to let myself gaze at the gently
moving and flickering flame for a few moments after lighting the candle
and breathe in the beautiful scent of the essential oils that slowly drift
through the room. If you use incense, you might like to also find a nice
holder and make the process of burning incense something special.
On the other hand, if essential oils are your thing, try taking three deep
breaths to breathe in the aromas. I once visited an essential oil store in
New York, Saje, and upon applying a lavender and peppermint blend
to my wrists, the sales assistant invited me to take three deep breaths
to settle into my body. This was five years ago, yet the memory of this
moment stays with me. I think that speaks volumes about the power of
breathing and the power of smell.

Working with Music

As I write this sentence, I am sitting with my candle burning, tea
brewed, and noise-cancelling headphones on with John Mayer's
acoustic songs on repeat. I always find that listening to music that can
evoke a feeling of calm or even moodiness helps me settle into the

work zone. My go-to playlists for writing include "Cosy Jazz," "Jazz in the Background," "Lo-Fi Beats," and "Background Music." I also love a lot of older classics by Etta Jones, Leon Bridges, Frank Sinatra, and The Beatles. Many writers use the same playlist or song on repeat while writing. Everyone's preference is different, so you might like to try out a few different playlists such as lo-fi beats, classical, jazz, or binaural beats for focused work. My face now feels naked if I'm not wearing my headphones and listening to music while working. The act of taking them out of their case and placing them over my ears has become an essential part of my pre-work routine.

 I've created a special productivity playlist for you that includes songs from my favourite artists. You can listen on Spotify by searching for the playlist "StudyWithJess." I hope you enjoy it!

While these are my favourite three rituals to incorporate, there are many more. Importantly, you want to rely on rituals that can be done at home and in the office. You want your starting rituals to be portable and easily accessible, regardless of where you work.

Here's a look at my pre-work routine and how I incorporate starting rituals to build momentum and ease into a task without resistance:

* Brew an organic loose-leaf tea

* Make myself a hot water bottle (at home) or heat pack (in the office) during colder months

* Light a candle (at home) or apply a travel-sized essential oil roller (for the office)

* Select a playlist and listen to music with my noise-cancelling headphones

  * Put on my reading glasses

  * Set out my laptop and notepad

* Put my phone away

* Turn off the Wi-Fi connection (if I'm not using it, such as during a writing session)

What rituals do you incorporate into your work sessions to enhance your productivity and help you enter a state of flow? Note them below.

_____

_____

_____

_____

_____

_____

_____

_____

_____

Examples of additional starting rituals that you can do anywhere, anytime, to help you find your flow:

Make herbal tea	Five minutes of mindful meditation	Put on noise-cancelling headphones
Take three deep breaths	Tie your hair back in a topknot or ponytail	Drive to your workspace (e.g., the office, library, or café)
Burn some incense	Write your focus for the session and display it	Recite a positive affirmation
Select a calming music playlist	Diffuse an essential oil (peppermint or lemongrass)	Check your schedule or diary
Light a candle	Make a hot water bottle/ heat pack (in winter)	Prepare a snack
Turn off your internet connection on your laptop (if you don't need it)	Set out your laptop and stationery	Turn your phone on silent

Using the table provided, circle any starting rituals you'd like
to incorporate into your work sessions to help prime your mind
for productivity.

Feel free to come up with your own rituals. You might like to
choose one to five different starting rituals to incorporate into
your work routine, depending on how time-consuming they are.
The intention is to choose a couple of activities that you'd find most
enjoyable and that you believe will effectively help you feel calmer
so that you can focus and get to work. Remember, we experience
the greatest amount of resistance or friction to starting a task before
we begin. In pairing the same sequence of activities together before
you work, you are creating a new neural pathway in your brain that
says: tea + candle + noise-cancelling headphones = time to work.
Essentially, you are establishing a new productivity habit. This is also
why I encourage you to be consistent with your rituals so that this
connection is strengthened over time and you can more easily enter a
state of flow.

PART 3:

Barriers to Flow

CHAPTER 6:

Overcoming Distractions

"Time is what we want most, but what we use worst."

–William Penn

As I previously mentioned when outlining the concept of flow, the ideas and exercises found throughout this book are strategically set out so that each chapter builds on the concepts outlined before, creating a step-by-step framework for helping you to maximise your overall level of productivity. I believe that in this busy age, to have sufficient time off and fully enjoy it requires you to work at your most efficient and productive level.

By now, you've embraced the importance of creating an optimal morning routine to set up for the day ahead. You've gained clarity around your ideal working environment and the elements conducive to productive work. You've also planned out your new and improved work schedule to intentionally focus your energy on your top priorities and most mentally taxing tasks. Furthermore, you've put together a list of rituals and habits that you plan to incorporate at the beginning of your work routine to help you get into the work zone and enter a state of flow more easily. These carefully thought-out routines and rituals form the foundation for better work-life balance, enabling you to intentionally plan your days, begin your mornings with greater focus, mental clarity, and wellbeing, and assist in deeper levels of productive work while experiencing a greater sense of ease and enjoyment.

It's now time to address the common obstacles to productivity, namely any unhealthy habits and behaviours you may have developed over time, along with the many distractions and time-wasters of your external environment that can make it challenging to remain in a state of flow while you work and sabotage work-life balance. Without acknowledging these prevalent barriers, it's easy to fall off track and not see the full benefits and results of the work you've done so far. If left unaddressed, these obstacles can also lead to increased anxiety and stress, as well as poorer quality work and overall performance, so it's imperative that we cover them now.

If you're familiar with my first book, *The High School Survival Guide*, you might remember the little red bag tag story. When I was a teenager, my mum put her creativity hat on and made a "do not disturb" sign for my door. From memory, it was a spare red bag tag and she thought to switch out the card with our home address for a little piece of paper that she'd cut to size and wrote, "do not disturb, studying in progress." Whenever I'd sit down to study at my desk, I'd place the red bag tag on my door handle so my family knew not to disturb me unless it was important. It gave me peace of mind that I wouldn't be interrupted and lose my train of thought. This story of the little red bag tag inspired me to design a set of "do not disturb" inserts, where readers could take a page out of my book (get it?) and stick one of the signs on their door or pop them into a spare bag tag to hang on their doorknob while working. I recently read a book on productivity called *Indistractable* and was impressed when the author, Nir Eyal, mentioned his method for preventing external distractions. Like myself, he relies on a visual aid to notify the people around him that he doesn't want to be disturbed. He encourages readers to display a "screen sign" with a clear message above their desktop monitor. The sign is made from cardboard with an illustration of a red traffic light and reads, "Red light. I need to focus right now, but please come back soon."

Even to this day, I find it frustrating to be interrupted while I'm working, probably because most of the work that I do tends to require high focus and attention, such as writing this book or working on scripts for video content. My super tolerant, patient, and sweet husband, Adam, has been on the receiving end of my snappy comments and shoulder shrugs when we worked from the home office. I feel bad admitting this here, but he would often walk past me and interrupt my train of thought to gently pat my arm, come to give me a kiss, or simply say, "Hi, my beautiful," and I'd less than enthusiastically receive his thoughtful affection. Try that when I'm not deep in a task and I'm lovely as pie, responding with, "Hello, beautiful!" Basically, I'm a super nice person to be around, except for when I'm deeply focused on my work. Then, you get the less sweet version of me.

> **"Some environments are designed precisely to lure us into acting against our interest."**
>
> –Marshall Goldsmith, author of *Triggers*

One of the most frequently requested topics I get asked to cover is how to deal with distractions and, more specifically, how to stop getting distracted by technology. A simple scroll through the hundreds of comments on my YouTube videos over the years, and you'll see it's a recurring theme. A distraction is any action that moves you away from what you want and stops you from achieving your goals, even if momentarily. The problem with distractions is that they take up an unnecessary amount of time that we can never get back, forcing us to eat into our precious personal time off that could otherwise be spent tending to our needs and desires. While some distractions are easier to account for and control, as you'll soon see, others can be more difficult to deal with effectively if you don't have a deep enough understanding of how they originate and have not put in place the right strategies.

Before we get into the common forms of distraction and how to overcome them, it's important to first break down the sources of distraction into two categories: **internal** and **external** triggers.[1] Internal triggers of distraction originate from within us. They are instances when we voluntarily choose to seek out distractions to avoid the task at hand. They can feel like an impulse, where you give in to temptation. If you ever stop work to text a friend or make a phone call because something else came to mind, or check your social media, you've given in to your internal distraction triggers. These forms of distraction originate from a lack of self-discipline and are brought on by the internal desire to do something other than work. External triggers, on the other hand, are forms of distraction that originate from our environment or the things around us. They seem out of our control, although there are always numerous ways to control these, as we'll discuss in a moment. Some external triggers include hearing

---

1   In *Indistractable*, author Nir Eyal includes internal and external triggers as part of a four-step model for becoming indistractable.

your phone notifications chiming, your ringtone signalling an incoming call or text message, a colleague interrupting you, your pet scratching at you for attention, or the delivery person knocking on your door.

Whether the source of your fragmented attention is due to internal or external triggers, the effects of getting off-task can have dire implications for your overall level of productivity. We know that to be immersed in a task and operate at our peak productivity levels (i.e., to be in a state of flow) requires us to be free from distractions for long enough to enter this state. Once interrupted and our focus is broken, it can take a while to get back on task. Even if this interruption is only for one minute, it can take longer than one minute to find yourself in the precious work zone.

In all my years of researching ways to enhance one's productivity, one assumption has bothered me. We've been under the false impression that we should simply be able to sit down and focus, and when we can't, we think that there's something wrong with us. To focus deeply on a task for an extended time is not something that you can just "do," unlike how you can clean your desk, pack your bag, make your lunch, or write a to-do list. This kind of focus takes practise. We expect to turn on our focus like a light switch, but this is not the case. And our ability to focus for longer periods to enter a state of deep productivity is getting worse. Why? The answer is simple. We need to train our focus muscles. Like any muscle in our body, we need to flex it regularly and long enough. People who jump from task to task, fragmenting their attention and all too often spending their mental energy on unimportant time-wasters, will find it challenging to sit down and focus on important work when it counts. Think of it like this: You don't eat healthy one day a week or exercise once a month to keep your fitness or health in check. To see a real improvement

and long-term positive change, you need to have a regular fitness routine and a healthy diet. The same goes for your focus muscle. You can't expect to be your most productive self and in a deep state of focus if you don't regularly allow your mind to concentrate on one task at a time for long enough. When you regularly allow yourself to be distracted by others or your impulses, the impact reaches beyond the task. You aren't allowing yourself to flex your focus muscle, which creates an unproductive behaviour cycle that only *you* can break. You may have heard the term "weapons of mass distraction" because these seemingly harmless incidences and behaviours aren't so harmless.

Our distraction-filled environment may have something to do with the concerning rate of students and adults being offered ADHD stimulant medication to help them focus. Just last week, I met someone at a party who told me how she had casually been offered Ritalin because she is working on her PhD. I believe there is a place for western medicine; however, when we take medicine to mask the problem and do not address the underlying causes that don't require medical intervention, it becomes dangerous. These stimulants have also been linked to changes in brain chemistry and can result in various side effects such as anxiety, changes in risk-taking behaviour, sleep, and weight.[2] I am not saying that if someone has obtained a diagnosis of ADHD or has other legitimate medical reasons that they should not take Ritalin or accept medical intervention. I will leave that up to the individual, their family, and the professionals. However, studies find that somewhere between 14 and 38 percent of students use stimulants to help them study. These include Ritalin and amphetamines, such as Adderall and Dexedrine. Most people who find it difficult to focus do not have ADHD, yet they are living

---

2   A 2017 study by Robison and colleagues looked at changes in the brains of rats given methylphenidate (also known as Ritalin).

in an ADHD environment. Our environment has a huge impact
on our overall ability to focus, but when our environment is
full of distractions, temptations, notifications, increasing work
demands, and competing priorities, what other choice do we
have but to try and manage it all by jumping from task to task and
doing our best to consume as much information as we can, while
still knowing we can never consume it all?

As I mentioned, some of these forms of distraction are easier to
overcome than others, so let's start with those first. To help account
for many of the common and unwanted distractions caused by my
external environment, like interruptions, noise, and notifications, I've
come to rely on several strategies. Below are seven practical ways to
control common distractions predominantly brought on by external
triggers in our environment. I strongly encourage you to implement
all seven where possible for the best results and to regain a sense
of control over your work sessions, regardless of whether you are
in the office, a public place such as a café or library, or working
from home:

* Invest in a pair of noise-cancelling headphones (they often
  double as a great "do not disturb" sign)

* Display a "do not disturb" sign if you get frequently interrupted

* Notify family members when you plan to work and ask that
  you are not disturbed

* Work in a low-distraction environment such as a library

* Avoid studying in high-traffic areas such as the kitchen table

* If working from home, leave a note on your front door for
  deliveries, requesting packages be left at the door (e.g.,

"Please leave deliveries at the door. I am currently in a meeting. Thank you.")

* Put your phone on do not disturb, flight mode, or silent and place it out of sight

With your external environment now more conducive to staying in a state of deep focus, I want to focus on the most experienced and challenging form of distraction that many—if not all of us—grapple with from time to time. Left unaddressed, it causes increased stress, anxiety, and overwhelm, not to mention overstimulation and reduced attention span. It's not just a barrier to productive work but a barrier to work-life balance.

A few months ago, a friend was over for lunch to see our new place. I put out a gourmet spread and placed all the dishes across our long, rectangular, wooden dining table. When we walked into the dining room, our friend couldn't help but notice all the books displayed and categorised in our built-in wall unit behind the table. It's one of my favourite focal points in the new house because I love to style it with my favourite dishes, house plants, photo frames, cookbooks, and candles on the top four shelves, reserving the bottom two levels for my growing book collection. (Side note: I often film book reviews on my YouTube channel and share my book recommendations each year if you're interested in watching those videos.) For ease of finding what I'm after, I've sorted the books according to their focus on business/productivity, self-development, spirituality, or wellbeing.

In my business/productivity section are two bright yellow books that caught his eye. These books were *Indistractable* and *Hooked* by Nir Eyal. We started talking about how companies strategically design their apps and websites to keep you scrolling and engaged for as long as possible and manage to get their users dependent on their devices and seek more stimulation. These companies have employed experts to ensure their products can maintain a person's engagement for as long as possible. To put it bluntly, the more people use the platform and the longer they remain on the platform, the more money these companies make. Instagram and Pinterest's scrolling features are strategically designed to play on our curiosity and our need to know what else is out there by revealing the top of the next image. The refresh feature that requires you to swipe down came from the all-too-familiar feature of a slot machine, which has kept gamblers hooked for years. Then there's the app notifications that, when paired with a unique pinging sound, create a compulsive need to check our phone and receive a fleeting "happy hit" of dopamine. Social media and the internet may be changing the way our brains are wired, with smartphones having introduced this habitual checking behaviour, whereby we engage in quick but frequent inspections of our device for incoming information such as the news, social media posts, or text messages. These self-conditioned habits happen when we receive "information rewards" that act as reinforcements for the behaviours. When we check our phones and access the new information, this reward releases dopamine to the brain, making us feel good. These feelings of excitement are fleeting, leaving us wanting more shortly afterwards and contributing to constant stress, making it difficult to focus or concentrate on other tasks. As I mentioned the importance of having healthy boundaries around tech usage, especially because it can negatively impact our overall attention span and focus, he shared something concerning. He told me that a few weeks ago, our mutual friend admitted that he used his phone while watching TV because TV no longer felt stimulating enough. I could relate, admitting that I no longer have my phone near me when watching TV because I previously kept catching myself scrolling on my phone at the same time and then needed to rewind my show because I kept missing important parts. What concerned me was that this issue is becoming more common, and while my friends and I didn't grow up needing to monitor our tech usage during high school, I am concerned for today's students.

Now, I'm not anti-social media, especially given my line of work—social media has formed the foundation of my career and the many opportunities I've had to help others and make a positive difference. However, I do advocate for conscious consumption. Undoubtedly, social media can be a valuable means for self-expression, accessing information, knowledge, and tools for education, overcoming physical barriers to connection, and even establishing a business. The danger arises when we fail to implement the necessary boundaries around our online consumption and truly understand the addictive nature of these products. The problem is that we live in a hyperconnected and overstimulated world, where we feel the compulsive need to fill any downtime by checking our devices. We aren't allowing our minds to function optimally because we bombard our brains with a constant flow of information. This means we are often multitasking or trying to focus on one task and hopping on and off our devices throughout the entire time. For example, you sit down to write an essay or a report and during that two-hour timeframe, you get a text, you answer a call, you feel the need to check your social media, you quickly check and reply to an email, and you find yourself looking up something unrelated on the internet. This frequent checking is not just evident when we are trying to work. People wait in a queue or wait for a friend at a café and can't help but check their phones to pass the time. Even waiting for the kettle to boil or the microwave to beep has become an invitation to quickly check our phones. This overstimulation can easily cause feelings of overwhelm in our day to day lives and is bad for our overall ability to focus and remain on task for long enough to enter a deeper state of productivity. This regular checking and multitasking distracts us from completing what's important, impacts our brains, and results in a shorter attention span. This makes it harder to stay on task, increases overall stress levels because we're overstimulated, and makes it difficult to practise self-discipline and sit down and work.

In one of my first Industry Level workshops at VidCon, the world's largest convention for digital creators, the speaker told us that our content needs to be engaging and have a hook within the first three seconds to capture the audience's attention and entice them to continue watching. This expert-recommended timeframe of three seconds has since been reduced to as little as 0.3 of a second when creating engaging video content on apps like Instagram. The increasingly shorter digital content we see online reflects our shrinking attention span. I remember sitting next to Adam one evening a few years ago when TikTok was the newest craze and watching him scroll through fifteen-second video after fifteen-second video, racking up dopamine hit after dopamine hit. Social media is designed to be addictive and compete for our focus and attention throughout the day, and our behaviours and preference for shorter content are informing the increase in the sheer number of more bite-sized videos and clips we see online. A study conducted by Microsoft found that the average human attention span is at an all-time low. In 2000, a human's attention span was around twelve seconds. According to their study, it has since dropped to eight seconds, which is one second lower than the attention span of a goldfish. One of the main reasons attention spans are falling is because content is increasing in volume. This dramatic increase in content exhausts our attention and need for new information. As a result, we've trained ourselves to focus on things for shorter bursts of time to move on to the next thing and regularly switch between topics.

Consuming more than one hour a day of screen time has been associated with lower psychological wellbeing, including more distractibility and inability to finish tasks.[3] The more frequently you use these platforms and the more you engage in daily checking, the more you impair your ability to focus on tasks for longer periods. Of course, there's a difference between intentional consumption and mindless consumption, as well as the type of content you are consuming and the timing of that consumption. Watching an inspiring twenty-minute talk on YouTube, listening to a guided online meditation or an interesting podcast before work to lift your spirit and energy, or doing a forty-five-minute online yoga or Pilates workout to begin your morning routine won't have the same negative effects as scrolling through thirty-second videos on social media for an hour, or checking whether anyone commented on your most recent post online when you're in the middle of a work task.

An Activity to Spark Self-awareness:

During your next work session, monitor how often you engage in or think about engaging in online checking. This can include going on your phone, opening unnecessary browsers on your computer, checking your smartwatch, or other tech distractions. Either jot down what you notice on a separate notepad next to you while you work or place a tab on this page and write it in the following spaces.

---

3   A 2018 study by Twenge and Campbell explored the associations between screen time and lower psychological wellbeing among 40,337 children and adolescents aged two to seventeen years old in the US. They included comprehensive measures of screen time (including cell phones, computers, electronic devices, electronic games, and TV) and an array of psychological wellbeing measures.

_____

_____

_____

_____

_____

_____

_____

_____

I encourage you to write down every time you think about using technology for something other than helping you complete your task to bring awareness to how frequently these internal triggers arise during a single work session. After completing this exercise several months ago, during a single two-hour work session, I noticed I thought about using the internet and my phone four times. Reasons my mind told me I needed to stop work:

1. To check the tracking on a parcel

2. To check whether my video editor had sent through the latest YouTube video

3. To check whether it was two or three weeks since I last posted to my YouTube channel, to decide whether to schedule a video for tonight or next Tuesday

4. To check whether I received an email confirmation from the person building us a new front fence

If I would have had my internet connection on my laptop turned on and my phone nearby, I likely would have stopped work for each of the reasons listed above because of the ease of opening a new web browser and picking up my phone. I would have suffered the consequences and gotten off-task. While some reasons would have only taken a few seconds of my focus, others could have resulted in a lot more time being taken up. For example, checking to see whether my editor sent me the latest video only takes a minute; however, if I received the video, I likely would have wanted to click the link, watch the new video, which is approximately ten minutes long, and leave comments and feedback along the way. If I could resist the urge to click the link, I'd probably still be thinking about it while trying to get back to my work.

So how can you ensure that technology is serving *you* and you are not serving *it?* How do you control when you receive information and not hand over your power to your devices? In the following chapter, I will take you through the steps to get to the root cause of any unhealthy habits you've formed and how to successfully break these. First, here are seven practical ways to take back control and ensure your devices don't turn into time-wasters:

*   **Make accessible only what you need.** If you don't need access to the internet while working on a task, turn off your Wi-Fi connection and, of course, keep your phone on silent and out of sight. I always turn off my internet connection

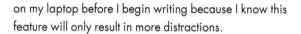

on my laptop before I begin writing because I know this feature will only result in more distractions.

✳ Schedule time for social media. I like to schedule time at the end of my workday to go on social media, whether to post on Instagram or reply to comments on my latest YouTube video. Scheduling a specific time to be on social media will reduce the temptation to check your phone numerous times throughout the day. Set an alarm or reminder on your phone to help you stick to your commitment and not use these apps outside of these set times.

✳ **Organise your apps.** I recommend organising the apps on your phone so that the first page features only the necessary apps that need to be most accessible. The weather app, Spotify, banking, calculator, reminders, and notes are all featured on my first page because I use these the most. Keep social media, games, and other apps that you find tempting on later pages of your phone to reduce the likelihood of opening them each time you need your phone.

✳ **Embrace the space.** How you use your devices outside of your work sessions is just as important. Avoid using social media as a filler when you feel impatient. If you're standing in line, waiting for a friend at a café, waiting for an ad on TV to end, or even waiting for the kettle to boil, don't reach for your phone. Learn to use these moments as a sacred pause in your day to notice the little things and take a deep breath. This will help flex your focus muscle and can be a simple antidote to the hyperstimulation we experience.

✳ **Keep a notepad next to you while you work** to write down important reminders as they arise. Do your best to resist the urge to act on them during this time unless they are urgent. This is a much better option than setting a reminder on your phone, which can be a temptation for other time-wasters and distractions.

* **Set tech-free hours** where you will commit to staying off your devices. I like to steer clear of technology for the first hour of every day and avoid it while sitting down for meals.

* **Create no-go zones.** Decide on locations where you will refrain from using your phone. You might like to make the dining room, bedroom, and going for walks your no-go zones to enjoy uninterrupted meals, downtime, and walks. This will help create a greater sense of calm and allow you to be present throughout the day.

I should also mention that I don't rely on any push notifications. If I am going to check social media, emails, or other apps, I've planned to check these apps when it suits me, not every single time a message, like, comment, or email comes through. Just last week, my mum complained that her phone was sending her so many notifications each day that it was overwhelming her and contributing to a poorer night's sleep. I went into her settings and turned off all notifications so that she no longer knew every time an email, WhatsApp text, or Facebook message came through.

CHAPTER 7:

Breaking Bad Habits

"Success is the sum of small efforts, repeated day in and day out."

–Robert Collier

I want to go even deeper into distractions, whether social media or technology in general, because I recognise that it is such a huge barrier to productivity, wellbeing, and work-life balance, and so many of us face this challenge daily. I want you to equip yourself with practical strategies for healthier and more mindful tech usage and ensure that you are getting to the root cause of any unhealthy habits you've formed over the years that are preventing you from getting the most out of each day. Even with the necessary boundaries around social media and technology put in place, you might still find yourself struggling to break these bad habits. While you put up more obstacles to make these bad habits harder to act on, we can't forget that many of the features of our apps, emails, and the internet make it difficult to not give in to these urges.

You can set goals to help reduce your overall tech usage, such as reducing the number of times each day that you check your phone, the overall time you spend on social media, or the time of day when you will avoid being on your phone; however, when it comes to establishing optimal and successful habits, I've found that systems are more important than goals. Furthermore, it's essential that you deep dive into any unhealthy habits you have developed and understand what drives them and how they impact your mood, focus, and productivity level. I've found that awareness is always the first step to making a positive change. How can you change something if you don't recognise it as a problem in the first place? I should also preface that while this chapter is designed to help you break bad habits around technology, the strategies can help you see positive behavioural changes in any area of your life. This includes unhealthy habits that have formed over time as part of your morning, night, and work routines.

Implementing positive changes comes down to the simple idea of habit formation. Once you do something long enough, it becomes a habit and somewhat second nature. You no longer need to put in as much effort as you initially did because the level of resistance you once felt has reduced significantly. For example, when I first began practising yoga seven years ago to keep active and reduce the overall stress levels that came with being a university student, it took more effort to commit to going to a morning class at my local gym across the road than to go to my local yoga studio now. I would pick out my exercise clothes the night before and leave them out to try and increase the likelihood of me getting dressed and going to class. I'd also register for classes online at the beginning of the week so that I couldn't cancel last minute if my reason the morning of was simply because I couldn't be bothered. I don't remember how long it took until I felt like I finally got into the swing of things and going to class became part of my morning routine, but from memory, it took a couple of months. I also think that going to the same classes with the same teachers and forming connections with other people helped make it easier to show up each morning and look forward to class.

Let's look at another example related to my previously unhealthy social media and work habits (ones I am not proud of). When I was twenty-five years old and had just started my business and YouTube channel, I would keep my phone on the floor next to my side of the bed. At the time, I was signed with an agency based in Los Angeles, whose time zone difference meant receiving emails and potential business opportunities during my precious sleep hours. I would wake up in anticipation to check my phone, read any new emails, and even obsess over how my latest YouTube upload performed overnight. I've always posted my YouTube videos around 10:00 p.m. AEDT (Australian Eastern Daylight Time), when most are awake and either beginning their days or getting home from school or work. Nowadays, I reply to comments the following day at a more reasonable time. As I previously mentioned, being on my phone first thing in the morning would mean that my mind would wake up earlier than planned in anticipation of new information. It left me overstimulated and overstretched. Breaking this bad habit and changing where I would leave my phone overnight, what time I would get off my phone each evening, and when I would use it the following morning took time, awareness, and self-discipline. At first, I thought about investing in one of those lockable jars that parents use as a form of punishment when their kids don't listen so they threaten to place their phones or favourite toy inside until the scheduled timer ends and the jar unlocks itself. Yeah, I was desperate.

The popular idea is that, on average, this process of habit formation takes about twenty-one days, although some argue that it can take several months. If only this easy-to-understand concept of habit formation was as easy to achieve. Sticking with a new behaviour long enough for it to become a habit or second nature is not something without its obstacles. If this wasn't the case, we'd purchase a gym membership and easily commit. We'd change our diets without a hiccup. Many of us would meditate daily, stick to a consistent wake and sleep schedule, never slack off from our workouts, successfully get through that pile of books we planned to read by the end of the year, and, oh yeah, stop checking our phones more than fifty times a day.

James Clear, author of *Atomic Habits*, details the four stages of habit formation and breaks down the psychology of behaviours, describing how our actions become habits. If you want to change your behaviours, then understanding how habits are formed will also help you identify how to break those habits that work against you.

Here's a quick breakdown of the four stages of habit formation that he outlines:

* **The cue:** The element that triggers the brain to notice an opportunity for reward or pleasure. The element can be several things, such as the sight of something, a smell or sound, or an interaction with another person or pet.

* **The craving:** The emotional relevance attached to a cue. When you notice the cue, the brain anticipates an opportunity to change your physical or emotional state. You begin to crave the pleasure that the change will bring about, and this craving is what prompts you to act.

* **The response:** This is the actual behaviour or habit performed to elicit the change you crave.

* **The reward:** The satisfaction or feeling of pleasure gained from the response. You have successfully satisfied your craving, even if only temporarily, and changed your physical and emotional state. A pathway from the cue to this state of pleasure is built through neural connections in the brain so

that every time you experience the same cue, the brain will be triggered to desire that same pleasure again. You will be prompted to perform the same action, creating the habit.

To put it all into practise, here's an example:

* **Cue:** You sit at your desk trying to work and look at your phone next to you.

* **Craving:** Checking your phone to see whether someone has liked or commented on your social media, sent you an email, or left you a text message will relieve the tension of not knowing and make you feel good by giving you a "happy hit."

* **Response:** You check your phone.

* **Reward:** You receive a "happy hit" and experience a sense of relief that you now know you haven't missed anything important and are fully up to date.

Identifying Your Unhealthy Work Habits

In the table provided, I invite you to list any habits you engage in during your work sessions that hinder your overall productivity and lead to increased procrastination or even stress. Writing these behaviours will help you become more mindful of your tendencies to block your efficiency and is the first step to overcoming these unhelpful habits. This might include multitasking, checking your phone, browsing online, engaging in conversations with peers or colleagues, or anything else that comes to mind.

My intention is for you to be bulletproof against distractions by creating an optimal work schedule and identifying any habits that hinder your overall productivity. Even with an excellent work schedule all planned out, we are not immune to the temptations of today's distraction-filled world. We have most likely formed several habits that break our attention and focus. It's time to break these habits and stop them from breaking your focus.

Let's create a plan of attack to help you identify the necessary steps needed to break these bad habits.

Unhealthy Habit	Motive	Reward	Negative Outcome	Cue

Unhealthy Habit	Motive	Reward	Negative Outcome	Cue

Identify the Motive

When it comes to bad habits that distract us from our top priority, it's important to address the **motive** or your *why*. Why do you engage in this behaviour? Do you want to keep up to date, stay informed, alleviate anxiety, or avoid boredom? Think about how you feel and your thoughts beforehand.

Get Clear on Your Reward

Next, identify what emotional or physical pleasure you desire? This is also known as the **reward** you experience after the habit takes place. Do you feel happier, excited, relaxed, or less agitated? For example, say that you have a habit of checking your phone in the middle of a work session to go on social media or see whether you have any unopened texts and missed calls. You feel restless beforehand, wanting to make sure you haven't missed anything important. Immediately after checking your phone, you feel relieved and happy. In this example, your motive is to stay informed and avoid experiencing the dreaded FOMO (fear of missing out), or you fear that a delayed response to a friend or family member might be perceived as you not caring about them. The reward is feeling relief, excitement, calm, or happiness during and after the behaviour.

Consider the Negative Outcomes

Next, consider the **negative outcome** of each habit. When you move your attention away from the reward to the negative implications, the habit looks a lot less enticing! For example, repeatedly checking your phone during work time has numerous negative implications on your overall productivity, mood, and attention span. Here's my extensive list:

* It pulls your attention from the task at hand

* It takes you significantly longer to get back on track

* It's a time-waster, resulting in your work tasks taking more time to be completed

* It uses up precious brainpower that could otherwise be devoted to important tasks

* Repeated phone checking shortens your attention span because you are not allowing yourself to focus on one task for long enough

* Frequent social media usage overloads your brain with additional stimuli and can cause you to feel more stressed and overstimulated

Identify Any Environmental Cues or External Triggers

Now, identify the **cues or triggers** that lead you to engage in this habit. This is about shaping your visual environment to help facilitate healthier behaviours and habits. For example, the sight of your phone or the sound of notifications are environmental cues that trigger you to notice an opportunity for pleasure. Go ahead and add these to the final column in the table provided.

In breaking down the elements that contribute to each unhealthy habit, you can take back control of how you spend your time and

implement the necessary boundaries to support your productivity. The aim is to use this newfound awareness, not to necessarily stop the behaviour entirely, but to stop the habit from interfering with your priorities. I'm not saying you can't check your phone, go on social media, engage in some online shopping or that you shouldn't play with your pets. There's a right time for everything. We simply don't want the habit of engaging in these behaviours at less-than-ideal times to continue. To help you do so, I invite you to try the following:

Consider how you can remove these external cues or triggers to remove the temptation to engage in each habit. As Marshall Goldsmith, executive coach and psychologist and author of *Triggers,* explains, "If we do not create and control our environment, our environment creates and controls us." Can you set your phone to silent? Place it out of sight so that it's out of mind? Turn off your Wi-Fi browser so that opening unnecessary tabs during a writing session isn't just one click away? Jot down your solutions in the spaces below:

> You might like to take inspiration from the seven practical tips I outlined in the previous chapter for taking back control and ensuring your devices don't turn into time-wasters.

Unhealthy Habit 1

_____

Ways I can eliminate unhelpful triggers:

_____

_____

_____

_____

_____

Unhealthy Habit 2

_____

Ways I can eliminate unhelpful triggers:

_____

_____

_____

_____

_____

Unhealthy Habit 3

_____

Ways I can eliminate unhelpful triggers:

_____

Unhealthy Habit 4

Ways I can eliminate unhelpful triggers:

It's also important to set boundaries. As I mentioned before, it's not about completely abstaining from engaging in the behaviour but rather engaging in it at a more appropriate time that works for you. For example, this could involve placing an alarm on your phone at a time when you will give yourself permission to check your social media. Setting alarms and reminders on your phone is also a great way of ensuring that technology works for you and that you aren't at its mercy. Having clear boundaries for when you will engage in certain behaviours also means you can enjoy them guilt-free.

Another effective way to break negative habits that have become reflexive behaviours is to take the period immediately following the execution of the bad habit and engage in a replacement behaviour that is easy to execute at the time. This behaviour needs to be a positive or favourable act that you engage in every time the bad habit occurs. While you could always try punishment—say flicking yourself with a rubber band or adding another dollar to a jar that you'll be giving to a sibling, friend, or colleague at the end of the month—opting to incorporate a replacement behaviour immediately afterwards has been found to help dismantle the neural pathway sequences linked to the bad habit. A meta-analysis by Fritz et al. called "Intervention to Modifying Habits: A Scoping Review" looks at various effective ways of breaking bad habits. Essentially, replacement habits create a temporal mismatch in the brain by changing the nature of the neural circuits, thereby weakening the strength of the initially formed pathway. Again, this is based on the premise that cells that fire together wire together. For example, you become aware that you just opened a web browser to check your social media again, even though you should be focusing on writing your report. Immediately, you drink a glass of water to form the positive habit of hydrating more throughout the day and consuming at least six glasses of water. Or perhaps you stop what you're doing, close your eyes, and take five long deep breaths while being mindful of your body. This positive replacement habit needs to be something that speaks to you and you would like to do more of.

Remember, breaking bad habits requires awareness and planning.

- ✓ Identify why this habit has formed and what it intends to do. It's important to be mindful of the positive (despite fleeting) feelings that the habit elicits, making it hard to break.
- ✓ By acknowledging the negative impact that this behaviour is having on your life, you gain awareness of this not-so-harmless behaviour.
- ✓ Only then can you begin to use this newfound awareness to create a more supportive environment that facilitates healthier behaviours by creating a written plan and removing triggers or external cues.
- ✓ All these steps will help support your intention for positive change and overcome the more challenging distractions we experience when trying to get our best work done. That means improved focus and attention, which ultimately leads to greater productivity and efficiency, which results in more time to enjoy life.

CHAPTER 8:

Overcoming Procrastination

"If it weren't for the last minute, nothing would get done."

–Rita Mae Brown

Now that we've sufficiently covered how to control common distractions and take back control from technology, there's still one other significant obstacle to productivity that needs to be addressed: procrastination. If left untreated, the procrastination bug can eat into your precious personal time and leave you feeling off in the work-life balance domain. While distractions are common for procrastination, they aren't the only reason. In this section, we'll explore the common causes of procrastination and remedies to overcome this unhelpful, unproductive behaviour. Whether you only occasionally procrastinate or have taken it up like a newfound hobby, this section will help you identify the root cause of why you procrastinate to get your work done sooner and without the added feeling of dread.

To put it simply, procrastination is when you choose to put off doing something, even though logically, you expect that in doing so, you will be worse off. It's also important to distinguish that while everyone

procrastinates from time to time—myself included (shocker)—not everyone is a chronic procrastinator. Procrastination within the workforce is a widespread issue, with as many as 88 percent of people admitting that they procrastinate at least one hour a day.[4] This might sound like an exaggeration, but if you factor in the unnecessary bathroom break, a trip to the kitchen to make a cup of tea that soon turns into an extended chat with a colleague, and a little online shopping, texting, or social media scrolling, you can see how easy it can be to clock up an hour's worth of time-wasting each day. Procrastination is common amongst students as well. A meta-analysis by Steel on the possible causes and effects of procrastination found that approximately 50 percent of college students say that they procrastinate in a consistent and problematic manner, approximately 70 percent consider themselves to be procrastinators, and approximately 80–95 percent engage in procrastination to some degree. I'd probably fall somewhere in that last category since I remember putting off an assignment here or there by a couple of days when I was a student, but procrastination has never been my default.

One excuse people often give as to why they procrastinate is that they work better at the last minute under pressure. There is, however, no evidence that actively procrastinating to create this time pressure produces better outcomes. Often, leaving things to the last minute can result in poorer quality work. This is not the only lie we tell ourselves when we procrastinate. We say things like, "I'll feel more like doing this tomorrow," even though when tomorrow comes around, it does not bring with it a newfound level of motivation to get working. I do, however, validate one's need for structure and a clear deadline. If we are given too much freedom, we will likely continue to put something

---

4   A study by Darius Foroux found that 88 percent of the adult participants surveyed admitted to procrastinating for at least one hour a day on an average day.

off since we don't give it a label of urgency. Instead, other more enjoyable tasks and time-sensitive commitments take precedence. If you are using the absence of an approaching deadline as an excuse to procrastinate, try setting yourself time goals. Break the task into smaller parts and schedule them in a work calendar and set mini due dates. These time-sensitive goals could be for the end of the week, day, afternoon, or even thirty-minute increments. Refrain from looking at the project that may not be due for several weeks still and instead utilise a project timeline to provide you with more structure and hold you accountable.

When Adam was in his previous job, he mentioned finding it easier to feel motivated working on a task when he was given an approaching deadline. He admitted that he can be a lot more efficient days before a piece of work is due because this is when he knows he needs to apply himself and get the job done. If he only needs a few days to do something but he is given several weeks, he'd likely do most of his work closer to the deadline. I have a friend of mine who is similar in her work approach. We worked together on my web series *Life of Jess* when she shared with me that she tends to work intensely and pull late nights as deadlines approach. I thought that so long as she was getting her work done and her work approach wasn't negatively impacting the series, it was no problem. As her friend, however, I was concerned about what the late nights and adrenaline would do to her wellbeing. On the other hand, let's just say I am too much of a type-A personality to walk so close to the edge. If I am given a deadline of three weeks, trust that *almost* always (almost, because I do admit to having procrastinated in the past), I will make sure to create a plan of attack, break the task into smaller parts, and schedule everything in my monthly work calendar. When I was in year eleven, every Monday, our teacher would assign us a

weekly essay to write. After class, I would carry my textbooks and walk to the library, where I'd find a silent room upstairs to work. You could find me there during my free periods with my head buried in my open notebook and my bright coloured stationery and textbooks nearby. On occasion, my friends would also find me there during the second half of my lunch break. I would usually spend the first few days of the week working on my essay so that by midweek, I knew I didn't need to worry about it and that I was successfully balancing my incoming and outgoing pile of assignments. At first, my teacher was surprised by my early submissions, questioning whether I was rushing and should take my time. He realised soon into the semester that this was my work approach and that getting my assignments done early was my way of feeling more in control of my busy life. In *The High School Survival Guide*, I shared how I was also pursuing my passion for dance, dancing over fifteen hours a week in the city after school and on weekends. My vibrant and busy schedule made me feel like I needed to have a good grip on my work and why I couldn't afford to procrastinate. They say, after all, if you want something done, give it to a busy person.

"Procrastination is the thief of time. Collar him."

–Charles Dickens

Practical tips to stop procrastinating *now*:

1. Eliminate all possible distractions

2. Set yourself deadlines by creating a project timeline

3. Schedule all work tasks and deadlines into your calendar

4. Prioritise your tasks so that you don't procrastinate with unimportant and nonurgent tasks that seem easier or more enjoyable

5. Reward yourself after you finish a large assignment or piece of work

Not always do we procrastinate because of a lack of motivation or the absence of a clear deadline. I invite you to mindfully read through the following section and consider which reasons for procrastinating resonate with you most. Perhaps one reason stands out to you.

* **Burnout.** Burnout or exhaustion is a huge reason for procrastination and one that I am familiar with. This is your body's way of saying that you need a break because it is physically and mentally starting to shut down. This can be due to taking on too much without getting enough rest, going through a significant and stressful period in life, or even being brought on by overstimulation from technology and feeling like you're always "on."

* **Fear of failure.** People often procrastinate because they are afraid to fail at a task and want to avoid experiencing shame or embarrassment. Low self-esteem and low self-confidence are associated with an increased fear of failure; however, even people who often believe in themselves and their capabilities can still experience a fear of failure around specific tasks. This is especially true if someone's fear is linked to a past "failure" on a similar task, where they were put down or told off by someone else. Fear of failure is also common in people who consider themselves to be perfectionists since anything that falls short of their perfect standards would be considered unacceptable for them to submit ("I can't mess this up; it has to be perfect").

* **Overwhelm.** Procrastination is also a common response when the task seems too big and has no clear end. For

example, it can be overwhelming to think about having to write an entire 40,000-word thesis as part of your postgraduate degree studies. While you know you need to complete this assignment, it seems like a huge undertaking, and it can be difficult to see how you will ever get to the end goal.

* **Unfamiliar.** In this instance, the task you're faced with is new, unfamiliar, and requires you to use skills that you don't normally use. Maybe you aren't tech-savvy and need to learn a new software system. Perhaps you're least strong subject in university is maths, yet you are required to take a compulsory statistic unit as part of your degree (this happened to me when I enrolled in my psychology undergraduate diploma). When faced with a task that seems out of your comfort zone and usual skill set, you might find yourself procrastinating in response to feeling hopeless or helpless.

A helpful exercise for identifying your procrastination "why" or root cause:

* Take some time to carefully answer the following prompts. Using the space provided, reflect on previous accounts of procrastination as you begin to identify insightful patterns and gain a greater level of awareness behind the root cause of your behaviour.

How soon after receiving a task do you typically begin working on it? Do you act immediately? Wait a few days? Or wait until the last minute?

_____

_____

_____

_____

What were the last three tasks you put off (for an hour, a day, a week, or even months)?

_____

_____

_____

_____

What did these tasks have in common? Perhaps they were all unfamiliar, large, or coincided with burnout. See what sort of similarities you can draw from them.

_____

_____

_____

_____

What was the negative self-talk or narrative you told yourself when faced with these tasks? E.g., "I can't do this," "I don't know where to start," "I mustn't fail or I will be humiliated," "I'm too tired to focus," etc.

_____

_____

_____

_____

"You may delay, but time will not."

–Benjamin Franklin

I've never liked the oversimplified advice people give when it comes to procrastination. The idea of simply conjuring up an additional dose of self-discipline and sitting down to work when you had planned isn't a holistic enough approach for me. Having a consistent work schedule, minimising distractions, and scheduling your tasks are all important ways to reduce your likelihood of procrastinating; however, for some of us, this response is due to deeper underlying reasons that deserve to be acknowledged.

With your newfound awareness of what triggers your procrastination response, it's time to take some actionable steps to address the root cause and explore different remedies. I've also turned this into an easy-to-read table at the end of this chapter that summarises the following information so that you can glance over it any time and revisit these helpful solutions.

Burnout

If you find yourself in the face of burnout or mental exhaustion, the first thing you should do is R.E.S.T. Too often we feel guilty for resting because we live in a culture that glorifies being busy; however, rest is essential for bouncing back from burnout.

R.E.S.T. is a handy little acronym I've created to help you remember these four important initial steps.

"R.E.S.T." stands for Reflect, Embrace, Self-Compassion, and Time.

* **Reflect** on everything you've done recently and that you have asked your body to do for you. Acknowledge all the mental, physical, or emotional load you've recently carried that has contributed to how you are currently feeling.

* **Embrace** where you are and don't try to resist your body's needs or your current situation.

* Practise **self-compassion**. Give yourself permission to nurture yourself and meet your own needs. Don't be hard on yourself if you feel like you took on too much. Use it as a learning experience instead. This is where you are, so there's no fighting it or kicking yourself for being in this place.

* Give it **time** and be patient. Healing takes time, but the body and mind will bounce back.

I also wanted to mention briefly that burnout is not a sign of failure. Burnout happens because life happens and we do our best to mindfully take on what we can, although sometimes our body is there to teach us to pull back and make necessary adjustments. Some things in life are out of our control, such as grief or navigating a pandemic; however, you can control how you respond to these things. You can control how quickly you tune into your body and notice your warning signs. How much resistance you put forward before you finally begin to prioritise yourself is up to you. Personally, my initial signs of burnout being on the horizon come in irritability or brain fog. Being able to pick up on these cues and take immediate action helps me prevent any further symptoms and restore my energy sooner.

If you notice yourself procrastinating because you feel mentally or physically too tired to get your work done when you intended, then here are some practical things you can do to better support yourself and bounce back and prevent future cases of burnout. We will also explore how to prioritise your wellbeing in more depth in the next section of this book, but for now, here are a list of solutions I encourage you to try.

Ten Ways to Bounce Back from Burnout:

1. Reassess your current workload and commitments.

2. Consult a life coach if this is a recurring issue.

3. Speak to your boss about your current workload and hours.

4. Take some time off to rest and recharge.

5. Build more rest into your day and prioritise this in your schedule.

6. Consult a health practitioner if you're feeling run down and perhaps could benefit from some supplements or vitamins. Also, be sure to get your levels checked and have a routine blood test.

7. Prioritise sleep and try going to bed earlier.

8. Avoid overscheduling.

9. Focus on your top priorities and say no to anything else while you get your energy back.

10. Identify the warning signs and take early and preventative action. Common early signs of burnout can include irritability, restlessness, brain fog, fatigue, lack of motivation, feeling sad or uninspired, or needing to sleep more.

Fear of Failure

Procrastination can also act as a protective behaviour that shields us from the possibility of failure and the associated feelings of shame, embarrassment, humiliation, and disappointment. If you are faced with a fear of failure, I strongly encourage you to reach out to your support to help you work through it. Speak to a counsellor or psychologist to address previous trauma around failure, such as memories of past humiliation. Sometimes, you'd be surprised how significant of a role a memory can have on our future behaviours and perception of ourselves. Someone close to me once shared that when they were a child, a teacher told them that they couldn't do something. This memory held a lot of power over them, and at times, they felt as though they shouldn't try as hard. I strongly believe that until we deal with the past, it will continue to have a hold on our future. If we truly want to feel free, it's important to face our fears and find the right people to help us work through them.

It can also help to remind yourself of previous successes. Unlike the many to-do lists we tend to create each week, it can be empowering to write out your own "I Did It" list, comprised of your past achievements. I should also add that this list is not restricted to your career achievements only. When we take the time to acknowledge all our "wins" and focus on our capabilities, it can help give us the confidence boost we need to push through our fear of failure and keep going. Side note: I also like to create an "I Did It" list at the end of each year as a nice way to recap the year and reflect on everything I have achieved and learned, both in my career and personal life.

I am also a firm believer in the power of language and the words we tell ourselves. Your thoughts have power and when we speak encouraging, loving and supportive words, we act as our own cheerleaders. Never underestimate the power of your encouraging words said to a friend, a loved one, or particularly, a young and highly impressionable child. They can have a profound impact, and the same goes for you. Although this may not get to the root of your fears like seeking professional help can, using positive affirmations is a great tool for managing fear. You might like to recite or write a few positive affirmations to remind you of your capabilities. Make sure that you use "I" language to will it into existence, such as, "I am smart," "I am capable," "I can do this," and "If others can do this, so can I."

Overwhelm

I easily become overwhelmed when faced with a large project or a long list of tasks that require my attention. One way I have learned to deal with these feelings is rather than putting things off, I break down the task into smaller actionable steps. When I was younger, I remember my grandmother sharing some helpful advice for working through feelings of anxiety, stress, and overwhelm. She asked me, "Jessica, how do you eat an elephant?" Jumping in, as she could see I didn't have an answer for her, she responded, "Still, one bite at a time." No matter the size of the task, it can always be broken down into smaller, more manageable bites.

I strongly encourage you to not only break down the task but to then create a project timeline and schedule each step in your work calendar to hold yourself accountable. One additional piece of advice I thought I'd better include here is to make sure to give yourself more time than you anticipate you will need. One of my favourite quotes from Greg McKeown, author of *Essentialism*, is, "We often overestimate what we can do in a day and underestimate what we can do in a decade."

Unfamiliar

There will always be new things to learn because that's life. If we no longer needed to learn anything new, try new things, have new experiences, or face new challenges, how would we grow? Life would otherwise be boring. Yes, learning new skills and taking on unfamiliar tasks can be scary, but these moments can also be excellent opportunities to learn that we are more capable than we thought and to continue surprising ourselves. There have been times in my career when I've needed to do something that challenged me, forced me to further develop a set of skills, and I didn't feel much like an expert at all. From cocreating, producing, and acting in a web series with no previous experience, to teaching myself how to film and edit my YouTube videos, or setting up a printer and new software for a brand partnership, I've been tested and (at times) wanted to put off doing a task, even for a little while. I found it helpful to draw on my previous experiences when I had to do something I didn't feel particularly skilled at, only to successfully get the job done. It helps remind me that the next time I'm faced with an unfamiliar task, everything will be okay. Try thinking about a time when you completed a project, assignment, or task that was initially unfamiliar and daunting. Also, remember your "I Did It" list? This is another great opportunity to remind yourself of your past accomplishments and reinforce that you can complete any task, even when you feel out of your depths and in new and unfamiliar territory.

One other way to avoid using procrastination as a coping mechanism in these situations is to make a list of supports you can access next time you receive a similar task. Remember, what might be unfamiliar to you could be someone else's piece of cake. As Adam likes to remind me, "You are not on an island." You can always seek support if you get stuck, so never be afraid to ask for help. People love to feel needed and often seize an opportunity to share their expertise. Is there a friend, family member, colleague, or someone else you can reach out to? In addition, making a note of various resources that you can always turn to, such as useful websites or textbooks, can bring added comfort. My initial go-to resource is usually YouTube since I find short, explanatory videos where I can follow a step-by-step process to be the most helpful.

Causes of Procrastination	Solutions
Burnout	* Reassess your current workload and commitments * Consult a life coach if this is a recurring issue * Speak to your boss about your current workload and hours * Take some time off to rest and recharge * Build more rest into your day and prioritise this in your schedule * Consult a health practitioner if you're feeling run down and perhaps could benefit from some supplements or vitamins. Also, be sure to get your levels checked and have a routine blood test * Prioritise sleep * Avoid overscheduling * Focus on your top priorities only and say no to anything else while you get your energy back * Identify the warning signs and take early action. Common early signs of burnout can include irritability, restlessness, brain fog, fatigue, lack of motivation, feeling sad or uninspired, or needing to sleep more

Fear of Failure	✱ Speak to a counsellor or psychologist to address previous trauma around failure
	✱ Reflect on your past success and achievements by creating an "I Did It" list
	✱ Use positive affirmations such as "I am smart," "I am capable," "I can do this," and "If others can do this, so can I." Write these down and display them on your desk or say them to yourself in the mirror each day
Overwhelm	✱ Break down tasks into smaller actionable steps
	✱ Create a project timeline and schedule each step in your calendar to hold yourself accountable
	✱ Make sure to give yourself more time than you anticipate you will need. Remember, "We often overestimate what we can do in a day and underestimate what we can do in a decade"

Unfamiliar	* Create an "I Did It" list to help build self-confidence
	* Embrace the unfamiliar as an opportunity to learn, expand your skill set, and grow
	* Try thinking about a time when you completed a project, assignment, or task that was initially unfamiliar and daunting
	* Make a list of supports and resources you can access if you need help or get stuck

One last quick tip for beating the procrastination bug: Don't forget to reward yourself. Rewards are a great way to incentivise yourself to work because they help build motivation and encourage self-discipline. Deciding how you will reward yourself after you complete your goals (whether it's submitting the entire piece of work or finishing a portion of it by your chosen deadline), will give you something to look forward to. I tend to choose rewards based on the level of work I have to put in. For small tasks, I like to reward myself with watching a movie, taking myself out for a chai latte, or grabbing a smoothie to enjoy at my local park. Larger tasks tend to be paired with larger rewards, such as getting a massage. Bliss.

PART 4:

Achieving Better Work-Life Balance

Musings

Today started differently.
Today didn't start on time.
Today was not a day for doing.
Today was a day for being.
Being human,
Just being.
I sat with my feelings.
I sat with my thoughts.
Today I tuned in,
Instead of tuning out.
Today would be for me,
And not for them.
Today I gave myself a break,
To avoid having a breakdown.
I thought about how I spent my day,
As though every day should be spent.
Spent doing.
Spent until we feel spent ourselves.
Today, I decided not to *spend* the day,
but instead, today was for saving.
I saved my breath.
I saved my energy.
Today started differently,
And it ended differently.

CHAPTER 9:

Making Time for Rest

"People say nothing is impossible, but I do nothing every day."

–A.A. Milne

This section is the one I have been most looking forward to writing for several reasons. I am so grateful for the opportunity to share my experiences, struggles, and lessons around work-life balance with you, in the hope that parts of my journey resonate with and inspire you to make positive changes. I hope you will freely give yourself the permission to implement the advice I am about to share with you. May it support you in building a life and lifestyle that is authentic to you and nurtures and meets your needs guilt-free. This book has also helped me to hold myself accountable, approach my work more mindfully than before, and make sure I pace myself in my writing marathon by not only staggering my work in a healthier and more sustainable way but also by sprinkling in more time for rest and self-care. This final section of this book is based on the foundation of the four R's: rest, restore, reflect, and reset. First, we'll focus on the importance of and interconnection between rest and productivity because as you'll discover, rest is an integral element for focus, creativity, and productivity. Next, we'll get into some of my favourite ways to restore your energy and bring more balance into your life. Finally, this section concludes with guided reflections to help you move forward mindfully, reset, and plan for another successful week.

I've had to learn the hard way just how important work-life balance is. Correction: I've had to learn the hard way *what* work-life balance is. I don't remember growing up and seeing work-life balance modelled in my home. I certainly don't remember hearing of work-life balance or self-care displayed in my parents' homes either. My parents were lovingly present, and they weren't workaholics, but my memories of them practising regular self-care and making enough time for rest are quite rare. I could take the "easy" way out and blame my workaholic tendencies on my parents, but to be honest, I am quite sure it's also in my nature. I was never good at resting and tuning into my body and it caught up with me in my twenties. Unfortunately, I had quite a few experiences with burnout, especially in the first few years of starting my business. Eventually (and unknowingly), I found my life coach, who has drilled into me the importance of rest and being more compassionate towards myself. I say "unknowingly" because the story behind how I ended up seeing a life coach makes me think that the universe decided to play a game and trick me into getting some help. I don't think I would have otherwise looked for a coach, at least not in my twenties.

Four years ago, I was meant to take part in a business development program for digital content creators. Unfortunately, the program didn't end up going ahead, but as a consolation, they offered me six sessions with a coach. I thought I would be spending those six sessions strategizing and carving out a

detailed plan to take my business to the next level, but those six online sessions over Zoom ended up being beneficial to my business *and* my wellbeing. We talked about my goals, values, and plans for my career, but we also delved deeper into other things like self-confidence, self-care, and burnout. Creator burnout is a huge problem and something that all other digital content creators I have spoken to have admitted they grapple with too. I think this is because in addition to the demands of running our own business and feeling as though our personal and work life are all too closely intertwined, we find ourselves in an industry that never sleeps and where we feel as though we could always be doing more. There's always something we could be doing—vlogging, posting, going live, the list goes on—and we fear that taking a break could see the collapse of our careers. We often find ourselves at the mercy of algorithms and feel the need to keep up, and this added stress sometimes stifles our creativity even more. Sometimes I still hear my inner critic telling me that I am not doing enough. In those moments, I try and take a step back to acknowledge everything that I *am* doing and remind myself that I am doing the best I can. I want to be creating from a place of inspiration and not from a place of self-comparison. This is also why I try not to pay too much attention to what everyone else is doing; otherwise, it can get quite distracting and make me forget that while someone might be livestreaming and posting videos weekly, they aren't also writing a book or juggling the same projects as I am. I think we all need to find the right balance and do what feels right for us. We each have different stamina, and we each recharge our energetic batteries in our own way.

My mum and I use a saying when it comes to the importance of honouring our needs and taking care of ourselves. I believe this saying came from my late grandfather, and when translated into English, it is, "If I am not here for myself, who is here for me?"

It signifies the importance of being there for ourselves and that we cannot expect others to completely take care of us. That's not to discount the support we receive from family and friends or that if ever we need, there will always be someone there for us to turn to. It's simply to remind us that we need to take care of ourselves first. We must be there for ourselves. We must put ourselves and our wellbeing at the top of our priorities. Besides, if you don't take care of yourself, how can you expect to care for others?

"The first wealth is health."

–Ralph Waldo Emerson

We live in a society that glorifies being busy. It sadly makes me question whether we value wealth over health. I mean, we value doing over being. Talking over listening. Working over resting. Striving over non-doing. The rest x productivity relationship isn't acknowledged, so many of us experience "rest resistance," whereby we feel guilty for stopping because we are concerned that we will be seen as "lazy." No one has given us permission to slow down in this fast-paced environment, so it's hard to grant ourselves that permission since we don't see the true value in rest. Know this: You do not need to earn rest. It is there for you to claim. I wish rest was favoured equally to output, especially since you cannot have one without the other. Doing and creating requires you to make time for rest. Sometimes the most productive thing you can do is rest. The simplest example of this would be when you sleep each night to recharge for the following day. Take a page out of Mother Nature's book too. Nothing in nature blooms all year round. There is one piece of advice that I've found most comforting when faced with this inner conflict of needing to rest but wanting to work. When I first heard my coach say this approximately a hundred times ago, it felt like it silenced my inner critic at that moment and I came home to myself. This advice is something I remind myself of weekly and often share it in my work. These powerful words have changed how I approach my life and the expectations I place on myself. These powerful and healing words are:

"You are a human *being*, not a human *doing*."

Simple, yet profound. I think it deserves a line to itself. Many people spend a large part of their life in an over-adrenalized state, feeling wired and tired. Not only is slowing down not encouraged enough in the workforce and certainly not in schools, but slowing down and stopping can also be particularly confronting because it requires us to stop running and to feel into our bodies. It requires us to face life honestly and show up for ourselves, not others.

When I was twenty-four I went to see a new psychologist after experiencing a traumatic incident. My first session was quite general, and we spoke a little bit about my work, childhood, and moments when I'd felt heightened anxiety. While we were talking, she said to me, "It sounds like you have a pretty strong Task Master." She explained that we are made up of different parts that must come together to help us navigate life and one of the parts that makes up who we are is our Protector, which can take on the form of a Task Master. This part of us tells us to sit down and work. To get it done. To achieve and do. When my body needs rest, my Task Master tells me I should do a little more. My Task

Master had been strengthened by all the praise I had received whenever I would achieve, and by seeing how much society valued "doing." Until my mid-late twenties, my self-worth was tied to my achievements, so when I wasn't achieving, I felt less worthy. I've had to work through this to get to a place where I can give myself permission to rest and honour my needs without feeling guilty. It's so important because it means I now prioritise my wellbeing over anything else, that I am more in tune with my body's needs, and that I can build in more time for rest the moment I need it, rather than getting to the point of burnout, which is when my body *makes* me rest.

My parents have also had to learn the hard way when it comes to the importance of rest. Their encounters with burnout have always remained in the back of my mind, cautioning me to take extra care of myself and learn from their challenges. When I was two years old, my dad had his first experience with chronic fatigue. A demanding work life, coupled with some significant stress he was under at the time, meant his body began crying out for much larger doses of self-care, rest, and self-compassion. I also recently learned that my mum had a panic attack brought on by extreme exhaustion when I was a little over a year old. She was trying to do it all and worked late into the evenings, attended weekly networking events for work, and came home as late as 2:00 a.m. After that experience, she decided to stop working for a few years to prioritise herself and her family. I've seen loved ones juggling two jobs and collapse in front of me. I've heard of friends' partners working seven-day workweeks and later ending up so unwell that they had to go to the hospital. I've had friends fail to prioritise their own needs while starting a business, so much so that they become bed-ridden for a week and rundown with a cold. These stories remind me that if you don't make time for health, soon enough, you will have to make time for sickness.

There's still so much guilt attached to resting. We need to stop making a connection between resting and laziness because it's not the same. About a year ago, I was speaking to my best friend over the phone about burnout and how, at times, I still noticed feelings of guilt creep in when I knew I needed to take time off and rest. I needed to temporarily say no to social commitments and family gatherings because I needed to focus on healing and getting my energy back after taking on some large projects that coincided with personal challenges life threw my way. My friend has a history of chronic fatigue, so I found it helpful to confide in her and find out how she manages to say no to commitments and yes to rest without feeling guilty. She told me that it got to the point where she no longer could justify giving energy to others and caring whether people understood her need to stay in and rest or not. Feeling guilty would just waste what was left of her little energy. There's no use sitting at home in pyjamas if you're expelling so much energy caring what other people think and whether you'll be perceived as lazy, flaky, or uninterested. It's counterproductive. Besides, true friends and loved ones should care enough to support you when putting your needs first. They should understand it's not personal and sometimes we need to step back and focus on ourselves. Some people re-energise by going for hikes, seeing friends, or letting loose. I re-energise by being in nature or staying in, wearing pyjamas, watching TV, and cuddling up with a hot water bottle and my dog Winston in bed. I'll plod around my house or garden, tend to the herbs and flowers, maybe do a little baking if I feel like it, but that's about it.

What are three things in your life that would change if you were well-rested? Take a moment to think about this. Would you see improvements in your relationships? Work? Wellbeing? Mood?

Mental health? Marriage? Mental clarity and ability to make better decisions?

1. _____

2. _____

3. _____

It's also harder to rest and allow our minds to switch off because we live in a hyperconnected and overstimulated world. We take our phones wherever we go, allowing our notifications to fool us into thinking every email, text, missed call, or social media update requires our urgent attention. Technology is taking up a lot of the space we otherwise would use to rest and slow down. Nowadays, if we so choose to, we can have a constant flow of information and be mentally stimulated and occupied 24/7. The result? Burnout. The idea of always being "on" means we are giving more and more of our energy and attention to these devices, leaving us with less energy for the rest of our day. We are burning through our energy faster because we are spending it more frequently, carelessly, and unintentionally. Again, this is why it is so important not to check your phone or be on technology for at least the first thirty, if not sixty minutes of your morning.

My tell-tale sign that I am feeling overstimulated or wired is my breathing. I've noticed that my breathing becomes shallower, and I find it hard to take a full inhale, almost like there's a tightening in my upper rib cage. I try to inhale deeply but I can't. When my breathing becomes shallow, I know I need to get outdoors and switch off. Within a short amount of time, I feel my shoulders, throat, and chest relax again. Since I spend a lot of time plugged in for work, I also take deliberate breaks from social media to allow my mind to rest. I

consciously don't take my phone when I go for walks to the park or when Adam and I take Winston down the coast to run on the beach. The absence of my phone helps me switch off, although there are times when I wish I had it on me. Whenever we head down the coast, we almost always see a pod of dolphins swimming close to shore— I'm talking so close that last week I exclaimed, "Oh my gosh, they look like they're about to come onto the shore!" I would have loved to capture it on my phone, but it forces me to live in the moment and make mental memories.

Here are three ways to thrive in a hyperconnected and overstimulated world. I invite you to implement all three, set healthy tech boundaries, and reduce the amount of noise in your day. This will help you to properly "switch off" and rest.

* **Create phone-free zones:** Establishing phone-free zones in the home will help you to be fully present. Ideally, these zones should be reserved for rest and connection, such as the bedroom and dining room.

* **Try a tech-tox:** I do this whenever I feel overwhelmed or like my mind is full of thoughts. A technology detox involves turning off my phone and laptop and staying off social media and my devices for anywhere between three to ten days to get the full benefits. Just the other month, my sister Michelle texted me to let me know she was taking a tech-tox over the weekend and that she would not be contactable. Letting loved ones know in advance can save them any worries if they can't get a hold of you.

* **Social media sabbath:** This is when you go social media-free for one day a week. No Instagram. No TikTok. No Facebook. No Pinterest. I try and do this every weekend as part of my overall commitment to live a mindful and slower-

paced life, so I can be present with my loved ones and enjoy my weekends to the fullest.

I also encourage you to learn about digital minimalism and the different ways to make sure all your devices and technology in general are serving you. There are many ways we can reduce our overall tech usage and make sure we are consuming information when we want and not being bombarded by notifications. While learning more about digital minimalism, I recently read about the idea of scheduling times to reply to texts and phone calls to not interrupt our precious resting time. It's easy. Place your phone on do not disturb—although your favourites list will still be able to contact you if they ring several times in an emergency—and this way, you don't end up checking your phone constantly and replying to texts each time one comes in.

CHAPTER 10:

Whole Living

**"Step with care and great tact
and remember that life's a great
balancing act."**

–Dr. Seuss

The term "work-life balance" embodies our need for productivity and rest. Too much work and too little rest, and we become exhausted and burnt out. Too much rest, play, and dreaming, and we might start to feel as though our days lack structure and purpose, not to mention we also need to make a living to sustain our basic need for shelter and food. The problem is that we are always in pursuit of work-life balance but never able to fully attain it (or at least, not for long). The ambitious part of me naively took it as a goal to successfully achieve and ticked off once and for all—like life is ever that simple! Each time I'd feel my life lean out of balance, I'd feel a sense of failure. "How am I *here* again?" I'd ask myself in frustration. Perhaps this is because when I try to visualise what work-life balance looks like, in my mind's eye, I see a pair of scales. This image tells me that for two things to be balanced (work and personal life), they must be *perfectly* balanced. Equal either in time, effort, or energy. It's that simple. It's black and white. Something is either balanced or out of balance.

Perhaps we are repeatedly coming up against obstacles to
maintaining complete balance because life *is* a balancing
act. Life keeps happening, and as a result, our responsibilities
change, circumstances change, and our needs change along
with them. We are not robots. What worked last month may not
work this coming month. As dynamic, flawed, unique, creative,
analytical, driven, complex (the list goes on) human beings, these
expectations we place on ourselves to be in perfect balance can
be counterproductive and too rigid, especially when we fall out of
balance and find ourselves in a situation where we need to reflect,
reassess, and re-establish a sense of equilibrium.

In the past, I've experienced burnout because I got caught up in my
goals and pushed past my body's messages and requests for rest, but
I've also felt exhausted because life can be unpredictable, and just as
you notice you need to pull back and focus more on your wellbeing,
you're faced with something unexpected, like grief, a pandemic, or
a loved one being sick. I want to emphasise here that our needs are
always changing. Sometimes we need more rest and self-care than
usual. There will be times when two yoga classes a week isn't enough
to keep me feeling calm and rejuvenated, and I need to build in more
rest to compensate for the mental energy I am investing into my work
or the emotional turbulence I might be experiencing in my personal
life. My bi-monthly massage becomes monthly or fortnightly. My eight
and a half hours of sleep each night extends beyond nine hours.

Sometimes we need more play and creativity, social connection,
intellectual stimulation, or physical outlets. Sometimes we are
overcome by a wave of passion or motivation and want to immerse
ourselves in our work. There will be times when ideas flow and all I
want to do is sit down and type at my laptop for hours, days on end.
A few months ago, Adam and I got into a deep discussion about

the negative implications of social media on young adolescents' self-esteem. Were these thirty-second dance videos with teens and pre-teens in short shorts or high-waisted sweatpants and crop tops sending the wrong message to young people about their sense of self-worth and body image? Is social media hypersexualising teens? We both had so much to say, that after dinner, I felt compelled to write it all down and formulate my argument. From 8:00 p.m. until 10:30 p.m., I wrote all my thoughts in an opinion piece that I later posted to my LinkedIn and social media accounts. This is not uncommon for me. Inspiration strikes at the strangest times and I've learned to just go with it.

I've noticed a shift away from using the term "work-life balance" recently, which is likely due to the language and the associated expectations or assumptions that can feel disempowering. You might even go as far as to say the idea of work-life balance is outdated. Instead, we're beginning to gravitate towards other terms such as "work-life flow," "work-life integration," or "work-life synergy," and advocating for a more dynamic and flexible approach to work and personal life. Something that doesn't reduce one's life to two components—"work" and "life"—helps us see our life holistically by acknowledging the many facets that make up who we are and our individual needs, passions, hobbies, and personal commitments.

"Work-life balance" is not a solution-focused term because it doesn't tell us exactly how to achieve this balance and harmony between the various areas of our lives. But maybe it's not meant to. Instead, maybe the purpose of this term is to reflect life's dynamic nature and the resulting need for constant adjustments and fine-tuning. It's there to remind us of the importance of our wellbeing and that we mustn't forget that our life is not comprised solely of our work if we want to feel in harmony with ourselves. There's more to life than work, and we need to consciously choose to adopt the mentality of "work to live," not "live to work." How we do this is up to each of us.

I'm not ready to give up on the term "work-life balance." I think there is a place for its powerful message, specifically when we consciously build a more sustainable and supportive lifestyle that enables us to be our best selves and achieve our goals. I am simply not ready or willing to discard it. Perhaps it is time for an additional concept or approach to life? Something that builds on this idea of work-life balance and fills the gaps. I spent a while exploring whether there was already a term that takes on a holistic approach to wellbeing (mind, body, and soul) and acknowledges the importance of one's career and the demands that go along with it. Terms like "work-life fitness" or "work-life synergy" didn't do it for me. I was speaking to my dad and sister over the phone one evening and put forward a new term that I felt would do our busy, multifaceted lives justice. I came up with the concept of "whole living." Whole living is inspired by a card I have displayed on my vision board that includes all the areas that make up my life and are important for thriving. It's called my "balance wheel" and I initially came across this concept while scrolling through images on Pinterest. My balance wheel acknowledges my multidimensional life: relationships, hobbies, career, intellectual stimulation, self-development, creativity, nutrition and exercise, and spirituality/religion.

Whole living is about integrating these aspects into your life and making sure you don't leave one out. It's not about having a set amount of time each day or week dedicated to a particular area but rather ensuring that you remain aware of the various areas that make up your life and make time for each in a way that suits you. There is still a need for flexibility on a daily, weekly, and even monthly basis when it comes to how we allocate our time. The focus is on intentional living. It's about listening to oneself and meeting one's needs by understanding that to be "whole" and function at our highest level, from a productivity standpoint and a wellbeing perspective, we must accept and respect that each area is an important piece of the puzzle. If you feel your life is veering off track, ask yourself whether a part of your life is currently missing or neglected. Ask yourself, "Where can I direct more of my time and energy to start to feel better?" When you embody the principles of whole living, you integrate each area based on your current needs, desires, values, and responsibilities. It's a way of living. Not an end goal.

I like to use the cake analogy to further explore what whole living is all about. A cake has several staple ingredients requiring different measurements. If you're anything like my mother or me in the kitchen and don't stick to recipes, you may find that sometimes you have a little more flour than milk or six eggs instead of seven. Maybe this time you want the cake a little sweeter, so you add three tablespoons of sugar instead of two. Regardless of the exact ratios or measurements of your ingredients, you still incorporate all of these ingredients because all are necessary for the cake to come out right. This goes for our lives as well. Depending on the day and how we feel, we may allocate different amounts of time and energy to each area of our lives, but each area is vital to becoming our best and highest-functioning selves.

My Balance Wheel

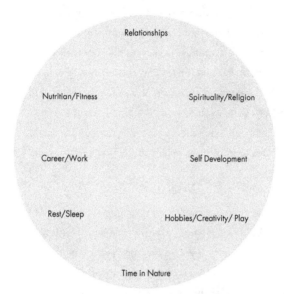

Relationships

Nutrition/Fitness   Spirituality/Religion

Career/Work   Self Development

Rest/Sleep   Hobbies/Creativity/ Play

Time in Nature

An Activity to Spark Action:

Use the space on the next page to create a balance wheel and
identify each area that makes up your life. My balance wheel consists
of eight areas: work/career, relationships (friends, family, and
community), spirituality/faith/purpose, time in nature, creativity/
play/hobbies, fitness and nutrition, rest/sleep, and personal
development/intellectual stimulation.

You might like to further break down each of these areas (e.g.,
"hobbies/creativity" might comprise of pottery, dance classes, and
candle making; "time in nature" might involve hiking, walking the
dog, picnics, gardening, and spending time at the beach).

To help you best allocate your time and energy, next to each of the areas, rate how much you currently prioritise or make time for each one. Assign each area a number out of ten (ten being you prioritise this area and devote most of your time and energy to it). Are there any areas that you have neglected? Perhaps you notice areas where you overindulge at the expense of others?

Acknowledging and improving each aspect of our lives will have profound benefits. When you begin to devote more time and attention to each area of your life, you will experience benefits. Tending to all areas of your balance wheel will help you create a well-rounded life. Importantly, you will also more easily be able to focus, be productive, and see success in your work life.

CHAPTER 11:

Everyday Self-Care

"Your job is to fill your own cup, so it overflows. Then you can serve others, joyfully, from your saucer."

–Lisa Nichols

One of my favourite sayings is, "You can't pour from an empty cup." I wish I could remember where I first came across this saying. It's almost as though it's integrated into my life so well that I never remember a time before I heard these words of wisdom. It's thankfully become a way of life for me. I even have this saying displayed on my vision board and have reused the same card that I found on Pinterest when searching for daily inspiration every year for as long as I can remember. It's a daily reminder to take care of myself and prioritise my needs before anything else. As my mum and I say, self-care is our much-needed "me time." Self-care is how we take care of ourselves and ensure we don't burn out. The benefits are widespread and the result is improved mental and physical wellbeing. When we practise self-care, we are practising a form of self-love. We are acknowledging our need for rest, play, and inspiration. We are tuning in and gently listening to our bodies. We are engaging in activities that are food for the soul. I came across a piece of writing a while ago and one line stayed with me. It read, "It's called giving yourself a break to avoid a breakdown." When we take time for ourselves and build a regular self-care practice into our busy lifestyle, we nurture and nourish our mind, body, and spirit to show up as our best selves in this life.

Self-care is quite a broad term. Initially, I used to think of self-care as pampering oneself. Self-care meant mani-pedis, going to the day spa, doing a face mask, eating chocolate, or engaging in other self-indulgent behaviours. I now realise that it's so much more than that. Self-care is also about setting healthy boundaries, being comfortable speaking honestly, and saying yes only when you mean it and saying no when you want to. It's about setting aside time for yourself, so that you can protect and restore your energy. It's working through and letting go of whatever no longer serves you and has been holding you back. It's speaking loving, kind, and encouraging words to yourself. It's about taking care of yourself, inside and out.

As you make your way through this chapter, you'll discover more ideas for daily self-care and ways to manage stress and anxiety and cultivate more calm each day. Before I get into some of my favourite forms of self-care and helpful exercises, I wanted to touch on the fundamentals or pillars of self-care. These are the nonnegotiables. The things that must, no matter what, be made a top priority over one's work, daily. Too often, I receive messages and emails from people who watch my YouTube videos, sharing that they simply don't have enough time to get their ideal amount of sleep each night. I understand that once in a blue moon, we come up against unexpected, last-minute deadlines or get thrown a curveball and need to work late. I've done this on occasion and then taken some time off to recharge once I submitted the work. The problem lies in prioritising work over our basic needs and the things that strongly contribute to our overall wellbeing. Getting enough sleep, eating three meals a day, staying hydrated, basic hygiene, and a little fresh air each day are essential and should always make it into your self-care routine. If you find it challenging to meet these requirements as part of your regular lifestyle, I strongly encourage you to reassess your commitments. Think about where you might be overextending yourself and consider seeking support and talking to someone, whether a counsellor, psychologist, life coach, teacher, or parent. I can't stress enough how important it is to look after yourself and make sure you aren't running yourself into the ground. Your health and wellbeing are the most important things.

I've noticed when trying to incorporate more self-care into my weeks that if I do not schedule it into my diary in advance, it usually won't get done. Simply committing to practising more self-care doesn't work. It's too vague and doesn't account for the fact that every day, we are faced with additional to-dos that pop up and other tasks that manage to make it to the top of our priority list and find their place in our schedule. Instead of telling myself that I will do something nice for myself *today* or treat myself to a smoothie and sit in the park *later*, I now make sure to schedule mini self-care appointments in my diary. I encourage you to give more thought to your daily self-care rituals and then schedule a set time for them so you know you are successfully making some much-needed and well-deserved time in your day for yourself.

While it's important to make time each day to enjoy the little things that fill your cup, it's also a great idea to schedule larger acts of self-care throughout the year. These larger and more concentrated forms of self-care become even more necessary following a busy period of work and can help prevent burnout. Sprinkling these special acts throughout the year also gives you something to look forward to. Think about how refreshed and recharged you feel after taking a week-long holiday or enjoying a little getaway? In addition to now taking regular weekend getaways with Adam and Winston down the coast, one of my favourite larger acts of self-care is treating myself to a massage at a beautiful day spa that recently opened in my area. Every time I visit, I leave feeling mentally and physically rejuvenated. Sometimes I don't schedule a massage for several months, although I try to budget for a regular massage when things get busy. Giving myself a big dose of self-care is especially important when I notice my workload increase significantly and I am taking on larger projects that require a lot more mental energy and time.

Easy ways to plan for bigger acts of self-care:

* Plan a holiday

* Plan several mini getaways throughout the year

* Take regular day trips to explore new places (i.e., parks, landmarks, restaurants)

* Schedule monthly massages

* Hobby for a term (e.g., a six-week pottery class, or join a team sport like basketball, tennis, or soccer)

* Commit to a weekly date night with your partner (go out or cook at home and stay in, whatever you prefer!)

Planning larger acts of self-care doesn't have to be costly. There are many great ways to enjoy a much-needed break that don't break the bank. Some of my closest friends love to go camping or take day trips to visit beautiful gardens, walking trails, or berry-picking farms. One of my favourite ways to spend quality time with Adam in the spring and summertime is to have a picnic at one of our local parks. Last month, we unexpectedly stumbled across free opera in the park that our local council had organised.

"As you grow older, you will discover that you have two hands, one for helping yourself, the other for helping others."

–Maya Angelou

In addition to having a healthy morning routine and being mindful of my work hours, my regular self-care practices help keep me feeling energised, inspired, and happy. When I take care of myself, I can focus better and produce high-quality work that helps others. I have enough energy in my day to get my most important things done and still be fully present in my relationships. When I prioritise my needs, I feel joyful, calm, and relaxed.

Here's a look at some of my go-to acts of self-care that I build into my schedule each week:

* Daily vitamins

* Eat a healthy diet of mainly whole foods

* Listen to my favourite music

* Legs up the wall for ten minutes a day

* Stretch

* Play with my dog Winston

* Weekly date night with Adam

* Gardening

* Treat myself to a smoothie/chai latte

* Walks in nature

* Skincare routine

* Yoga/meditation

A Little Bit of Solitude Goes a Long Way...

One of my favourite things to do lately to help break up my writing sessions is to treat myself to a smoothie or chai latte and enjoy it while walking through a local park. Just a short distance from our new home is one of the most beautiful gardens I've experienced. Every time I visit, I notice something new. I mindfully walk along the trail with a sense of wonder and light-heartedness. In the centre of the gardens is a luscious, lively rainforest. As I walk through the rainforest, I notice the temperature drop slightly against my skin. I hear the colourful Lorikeets happily chattering away and the sound of the mini waterfall flowing into the pond. At the end of the stream is a wooden bridge. As I stand over the bridge to look down, I try to spot the tadpoles beneath the soft growing algae that shades them from prying eyes. I linger for a while before making my way through the canopy. Next to the gentle stream of water is an archway formed out of the winding branches that have intertwined during their many dances over the years. Walking through the opening to the freshly cut grass, I always get a little shiver. The dreamer in me likes to believe that this would be the perfect hideaway and playground for little fairies to flutter about and play. There's something magical and enchanting about this part of the gardens. As I continue down the winding path, I find myself in the Indigenous Gardens, filled with hundred-year-old eucalyptus trees and other native flora. The local Magpies, Currawongs, and Miners sing their unique melodies as they fly between the trees, searching for an afternoon snack. I breathe in the air slowly and deeply as the sun warms me again. Nothing feels more like home than breathing in the smell of native Australian plants. Sometimes I'll wander over to a wooden park bench thoughtfully placed along the trail and sit to finish my smoothie or chai. Each seat is dedicated in loving memory to someone who helped contribute to the gardens over the years or would regularly visit. I find it heart-warming to read the plaques of each chair. For a moment, I stop and think about the impact this person had on their loved ones, the community, and the park. Then it's time to make my way back home. As I blissfully walk back towards the entry gates, my body feels lighter, more joyful, and more at ease. There's nothing more healing than time spent in nature.

55 Ways to Build Self-Care and Rest into Your Days

Take a gentle walk	Bubble bath	Legs up the wall for ten minutes
Read a magazine	Make a tea	Meditate
Light a candle	Sunbake	Stand barefoot in the grass
Take up a creative hobby (drawing, watercolour, pottery)	Bake something you love to eat	Sit in a café with a good book

Get a massage	Take yourself to lunch	Read an inspiring book
Meet a friend for a cup of tea	Go for an ocean swim	Go to the movies
Dance	Go on a date with your partner	Take a day trip somewhere new
Journal	Take your vitamins	Watch a comedy show
Buy yourself something special	Go for a hike	Plan a night in with friends
Stretch	Listen to music	Give yourself a hug
Make yourself a hot chocolate	Indulge in high-quality chocolates	Browse in your local bookshop
Listen to a guided mindfulness meditation	Practise yoga at home	Read a chapter of your book
Diffuse essential oils	Gardening	Cuddle a pet
Take a thirty-minute nap	Create a skincare routine	Relax in a sauna
Go for evening walks	Binge watch a TV show	Walk along the beach
Buy yourself flowers	Spend quality time with loved ones	Take a solo trip
Treat yourself to lunch	Paint your nails	Stare at the ocean
Make a green smoothie	Rewatch an old TV show	Take a staycation
Do a puzzle		

Creating a Self-Care Routine

Using the table of ideas, circle which rituals stand out to you, which you can see yourself incorporating into your daily routines. Feel free to circle as many as you like.

Next, in the spaces that follow, write down any additional forms of self-care you would like to regularly include.

I can nurture myself daily by:

_____

_____

_____

_____

What kinds of larger acts of self-care can you incorporate into your months? List ways to replenish your energy after busy or stressful times.

I can nurture myself throughout the year by:

_____

_____

_____

_____

Make sure you schedule your self-care into your diary or planner to make yourself a top priority every day.

Remember, self-care is not selfish. Self-care is essential. If you don't take care of yourself, how can you take care of others or show up as your best self at work? I've already touched on this issue of rest resistance and the guilt that many of us feel when we take time for ourselves, but I want to emphasise again how important it is to give yourself permission to prioritise yourself. It's time to stop wearing burnout with a badge of honour and lead by example. It's like the flight attendant always says on the plane, "Always put your oxygen mask on first before helping others." Over the last few years, I've noticed the growing self-care movement and that people are talking more openly about the importance of caring for oneself. Each time I walk into my local bookshop, I'm pleased to see a new book on self-care and ways to live more gently sitting on the shelf. There's also been a huge demand for more self-care content and tips online. People share their self-care routines on social media and post their favourite products and practices for taking care of themselves. It's great to get ideas from others, but remember that everyone recharges in their own way and what works for one may not work for another. Honour your needs as you listen to your body. If staying home in your pyjamas and rewatching an old TV show while doing a face mask brings you joy, go for it. If going hiking and disconnecting from technology fills your cup, get outdoors and breathe in Mother Nature.

CHAPTER 12:

Self-Care for Anxiety and Stress

"To meditate with mindful breathing is to bring body and mind back to present moment so that you do not miss your appointment with life."

–Thich Nhat Hanh

With the mindfulness meditation movement growing and the act of taking time to breathe deeply now becoming a staple form of self-care, I wanted to briefly touch on best practices for healthy breathing. Growing up, my mother occasionally taught meditation classes in the evenings. When she was a high school teacher, she also generously started offering free lunchtime meditation classes in one of the school's halls for the students. Her nurturing and giving nature meant that she wanted to help them manage the stress of studying for their final exams. From a young age, she taught me to breathe deeply and into my belly. She'd emphasise not to let my breath be shallow and stay at the top of my chest. She helped me understand that breathing in this way could help me feel calmer and more settled anytime I felt unwell, anxious, or overwhelmed. Importantly, there are different breathing techniques for different purposes. I've learned over the years—especially thanks to my yoga teachers who have taught me many different pranayama exercises—that the breath is a powerful and effective tool not only for improving our focus, helping us to fall asleep faster, or feel calmer, but for managing anxiety, stress, and depression. Deep breathing and mindful meditation can be like a gentle hug to your central nervous system.

I began taking a greater interest in the power of our breath over the last few years. I was on holiday with Adam and our dog Winston in the country and staying in a charming little cabin off the grid made from a shipping container when I first picked up a copy of *Breath* by James Nestor. I turned over the cover to read the back of the book and was fascinated to learn that we breathe approximately 25,000 times a day. Unfortunately, many of us don't engage in deep abdominal breathing. For many, the breath is shallow and rapid. When breathing at a normal rate, our lungs only absorb about a quarter of the viable oxygen in the air, while most of that oxygen leaves with our exhale. When we begin to slow down our breath rate, we allow our lungs to draw in more air. By taking longer, deeper breaths, we enable our lungs to soak up more oxygen for our cells to use, and we begin to feel more awake, alert, and focused.

Slowing down our breath isn't the only issue. Some people are chronic mouth breathers who either forget to breathe through their nose or tend to breathe through their mouth at night. As you discover some of my favourite breathing exercises that follow, you'll see that each should be practised by breathing in and out of the nose. I've grown up educated on the importance of nasal breathing, but it wasn't until I picked up a copy of *Breath* that I began to understand why this is so important. Research has found that nasal breathing alone can boost the levels of nitric oxide in the body sixfold, which helps to absorb around 18 percent more oxygen than we otherwise could when inhaling through our mouths. Our bad habits don't stop there, however. Not only do we tend to breathe incorrectly, sometimes we even hold our breath throughout the day without realising it. I once heard someone mention the term "email apnoea," a condition where we now hold our breath for short periods while checking and responding to emails. We are so caught up in our work that we forget to breathe. It's concerning to think that human beings have lost the ability to breathe correctly and along with our shallow and shorter breathing, we have forgotten the power of this healing tool that each of us possesses.

Learning to use breath as a tool for everyday life can be transformational. Here are three of my favourite breathing exercises to help reduce stress and manage anxiety. You might like to try each of them and see which one you prefer. Consider building in a few minutes each day to practise one of these breathing exercises and make it part of your regular self-care routine.

"Feelings come and go like clouds in a windy sky. Conscious breathing is my anchor."

–Thich Nhat Hanh

* **4x4 box breathing.** For this breathing technique, visualise four sides of a box or a square. As you inhale to the count of four, imagine you're slowly drawing the line for the first side of a box. Then, pause for four counts as you visualise the second side of your box appearing. Exhale for four counts as you draw the third side of your box with your mind's eye before pausing for another four counts to complete the square.

* **4x6.** This technique involves extending your exhalations to be longer than your inhalations and is an effective breathing technique to turn on your parasympathetic nervous system (the opposite of your fight-flight response, controlled by your sympathetic nervous system). Simply inhale for four counts, pausing for a moment at the top of your inhalation, and then exhale slowly to the count of six.

* **Breathing in thirds.** Inhale a third of your full breath into your lower abdomen or belly and pause for a moment. Then, take a second sip of air (about another third) and breathe into your upper abdomen, feeling your rib cage expand further. Pause again and take a final sip of air to fill up the rest of your chest before letting it all gradually go with a big, slow exhale.

"You should sit in meditation for twenty minutes a day, unless you are too busy– then you should sit for an hour."

–Zen proverb

Breathing Meditation

Start by taking a comfortable seated position and making sure your spine is upright. Begin to settle into your body, feeling your weight supported by the earth beneath you.

Place one hand over your heart and the other hand on your lower abdomen. Become aware of the natural rhythm of your breath without forcing anything. Notice as you begin to feel the rise and fall of your breath.

Notice any tension in your body. Soften your shoulders, maybe taking a little head roll from side to side and allowing tension in the neck to release. Relax your jaw. Allow your lips to be gently touching.

Anchor yourself by taking three slow, deep breaths, drawing the air in through your nose and directing it deep into your abdomen. Pause at the top of each inhale before letting it go and exhaling fully. With each breath, try to lengthen your inhalations and exhalations just that little bit more.

Rest the back of your hands on your knees or in your lap, with your palms facing upwards. Continue to draw slow deep breaths into your lower abdomen. Allow your mind to focus on your breathing.

Breathe in for a count of four and lengthen your exhalations for a count of six.

Continue with this simple breathing meditation for five minutes. To come out of this meditation, you might like to gently wiggle your fingers and toes, roll your shoulders backwards, and take a deep stretch with your arms overhead.

How does your body feel when you make time to slow down and breathe?

_____

_____

_____

_____

How does your mind feel when you make time to slow down
and breathe?

_____

_____

_____

_____

When in your day can you make time for breathing deeply?
When lying in bed? At a traffic light? Waiting for your
kettle to boil?

_____

_____

_____

_____

Heart Meditation

Find a comfortable seat or choose to begin this practice lying down.
You might like to play some relaxing music in the background to help
you settle into the present moment and feel a sense of calm. Once you
have settled in, notice your breath's natural rise and fall.

Begin to slow down the rate of your breathing, inhaling roughly to the count of four, pausing at the top, and exhaling slowly, allowing any tension in the body to fall away.

Now, bring your awareness to the centre of your chest, near your heart. Allow this area to soften and relax.

In your mind's eye, visualise a small, loving, pink ball of light in the centre of your chest.

Continue to focus your attention on this ball of pink light. With each slow, deep inhalation, imagine that it's beginning to expand, reaching beyond your chest, down your arms and legs, up and around your throat, and around your face.

Feel your body enveloped by the warmth and comfort of this light. Sit for a few minutes, noticing any sensations you feel throughout your face, throat, and chest.

Allow your heart to fill and expand with the presence of this pink, glowing light. *(Now that you are familiar with this exercise, try this visualisation with your eyes closed.)*

Were you able to listen to your heart? What message did you receive? Maybe the message was to stop running from fear, slow down, be kind to yourself, or be a reminder that you are safe and loved. This meditation reminds me that I am safe and a loving and lovable being.

_____

_____

_____

When we connect to our hearts and allow ourselves to get out of our heads, we can quiet our worries and thoughts. How did it feel to tap into your heart?

_____

_____

_____

_____

_____

Mindful Body Scan

I like to start this meditation by lying down, although you're welcome to take a seated position with your back supported and upright.

Begin by bringing your attention to your body. Notice how the earth supports your weight as your body sits in the chair or lies down. Bring your attention to what else you can feel. Feel your clothes against your skin. Feel the coolness of the air as it gently enters your nostrils and travels down into your lungs.

Allow yourself to be in this moment. Take a few deep breaths.

As you inhale deeply, feel the air circulating through your
body and awakening each cell. With each exhale, settle a little
deeper into your body and relax.

Bring your attention to your feet. Feel the floor beneath you. Notice
any sensations in your feet. Notice how your feet feel as they rest on
the ground. Can you notice whether they feel hot or cold?

Move your awareness into your legs. Allow your legs to feel heavy
and supported by the earth beneath you. See your legs sinking
deeper into the ground with each exhale.

Notice your back resting on the floor or against the chair. Continue to
mindfully inhale deeply, breathing in the feeling of being completely
supported. As you exhale, allow any tension to release and sink a
little deeper.

Bring your attention to your stomach. How does it feel? Does it feel
tense, tight, or relaxed? Allow your breath to flow into your lower
abdomen and, with each breath, begin to soften.

Let your awareness now travel into your hands. Notice any tingling
sensations in the palms of your hands or fingertips.

Now bring your attention towards your arms. Let your shoulders
be heavy and relaxed, melting towards the ground. Notice any
sensations in your arms.

Move your awareness to your chest. Notice the subtle rise and fall
with each breath.

Slowly move towards your throat and feel how each breath brings a sense of ease to this area of the body. Let each breath relax your throat and neck.

Notice the subtle tingling in your face. Feel your cheeks and lips soften. Allow your jaw to relax. You might even like to bring a slight smile to your face and notice how this brings a lightness to your body. Can you feel a warmth in your cheeks as you smile to yourself?

Allow your eyes to settle deep into their sockets, your eyebrows to relax, and your forehead to soften.

Now bring your attention to the crown of your head. Visualise taking deep breaths from the top of your head to the bottom of your toes.

Begin to notice your whole body present. Take one more deep inhale. Open your mouth and let it all go with an exhale.

When you're ready, take a deep stretch to awaken your body.

What changes did you experience from doing this meditation? Do you feel more grounded in your body? Calmer? Focused? Relaxed?

_____

_____

_____

_____

We rarely take time to notice and give our attention to each area of our body. Which areas did you experience tension? Were you able to release some of this tension during the exercise?

_____

_____

_____

_____

_____

If you're looking for guided meditations and breathwork, there are plenty of wonderful resources. My favourite apps include *Insight Timer*, *Calm*, *Headspace*, and *Smiling Mind*. My new favourite meditation app I have come across is one called *Balance*. Instead of everyone receiving the same meditation each day, the app tailors your meditation practice to your needs and provides you with daily recommendations. Also, a quick search on YouTube for "easy mindfulness meditation," "yoga Nidra," or "guided meditation" and you can find thousands of free online videos to suit your needs.

"I am not afraid of storms, for I am learning to sail my ship."

–Louisa May Alcott

Many of the breathing exercises and meditations I have practised have been taught to me by my yoga teachers. Over the past eight years, I've had the pleasure of soaking up the knowledge and

wisdom of my yoga teachers and learning new ways of quietening my busy mind through different breathing techniques. Yoga is also about pairing movement with breath. When I first began practising more intense or physically demanding active vinyasa classes, I noticed my tendency to hold my breath or let it become shallow when I moved into certain poses. My dance background had conditioned me to push myself, stretch as deep as I could, and for my focus to be more on how I looked in each pose than how I felt. It was stopping me from reaping the full benefits of my yoga practice. It took me a few years to break this habit and not care about how I looked or whether people were looking at me (they weren't, of course). I have learned that every single body is different. Everyone has different needs. Some people are working with injuries. Some people's bodies can move into shapes that others can't. I'm no longer there to compete or strive. I am there to breathe into each position and nourish my mind, body, and soul. Now, regardless of whether I am at the front of the class or grabbing a mat in the back of the room, I don't feel the need to look around. Instead, I look within.

Yoga has been a fundamental tool for cultivating more calm, managing anxiety and stress, and taking care of my body. It's helped me practise the art of non-striving and become more in tune with my body and feelings. I don't receive the same benefits and deep level of calm from stretching at home or staying active in other ways. I attribute a lot of this to the emphasis on breathing slowly, deeply, and mindfully. For myself, the benefits of my yoga practice have been many, which is why it has become a regular part of my self-care practice over the last eight years.

Each type of yoga practice serves a purpose. You might like to try a slow flow, restorative, or yin class if you're looking for gentle movements to strengthen and awaken the body, rejuvenating and relaxing poses, and deeper stretches. These are my favourite kind of classes to take each week and I find it easy to tap into my breath and slow down.

Here are my five favourite restorative yoga poses to relax:

* **Legs Up the Wall:** Place a folded blanket, cushion, bolster, or yoga block lengthways against a wall. Position yourself so that you are lying down on your back with your legs up the wall and your prop is supporting the small of your back. Place your hands over your heart or by your side with your palms facing up and breathe deeply in this position for five to ten minutes until you feel a tingling sensation in your feet. To come out of this pose, slowly bring your legs down the wall and back towards your chest. Either roll over your prop to one side and use your hands to come back up slowly or place your feet against the wall for support as you carefully push the prop out from underneath you. Again, roll over to one side and use your hands to help you come back to a seated position.

* **Supported Starfish:** Lie on your back with your arms and legs spaced apart like a starfish or like you're making a snow angel. Place a bolster or a rolled-up blanket horizontally underneath your knees so that your legs drape over the bolster and your heals gently rest on the floor. It can be nice to also place an eye pillow over your eyes while you enjoy resting in this pose.

*  **Supported Reclined Butterfly:** Place your bolster lengthways so it is in line with the length of your

spine. Bring the edge of the bolster right up against your lower back and hips before you gently drape yourself over the bolster and allow it to support your spine, shoulders, neck, and head. Bring the soles of your feet together and allow your knees to fall out to the side, making a diamond shape with your legs. If you find your inner thighs are receiving a strong stretch, you might like to support the outside of the knees with a block, cushion, or folded blanket on each side. To come out, use your hands to gently bring your knees back together before rolling onto your side and use your hands to help you back up to sitting.

Supported Bridge: Lying down on your back, bring the soles of your feet onto the floor, about hip-width distance apart. Reach your arms down by your side and see that you can reach your heels with your fingertips. Take a yoga block or bolster and place it horizontally underneath the small of your back. Make sure to position your prop so that the two dimples in the small of your back or the two hip bones in your back are supported. You want to ensure you're not placing any weight on the curve of your spine. To come out of this pose, gently lift your hips to the sky and slide the prop out from underneath you. (If you don't have a bolster, you can try using a rolled-up towel or forgo the prop altogether and still enjoy this pose and its benefits.)

Reclined Spinal Twist: Lie down and bring both knees to your chest. Give yourself a gentle squeeze and as you let go, open your arms out to the sides so that they are in line with your shoulders. Make sure your palms are facing down to the earth. Slowly drop both knees—one on top of the other—to one side. If your shoulders begin to lift off the ground or the twist feels too intense, place a cushion on the ground underneath your knees to support your legs. You might like to also turn your head to face the opposite way as your knees. After a few minutes, engage your core to carefully bring your knees back to centre and repeat on the other side.

Remember that with each pose, the aim is to feel supported and relaxed, and to focus on breathing slowly and deeply into your lower abdomen.

Mindful meditation, breathwork, and yoga are the main ways I proactively prioritise my health and wellbeing and reduce stress and anxiety. While I invite you to build these into your self-care routine and enjoy the many health benefits, I also acknowledge that many other forms of self-care can help reduce nervous energy and calm racing thoughts. It's essential that your lifestyle supports and nurtures your needs, so I can't stress enough the importance of making time to get outside daily for walks, eating a nutritious and healthy diet, taking any necessary recommended supplements, fostering healthy relationships, and getting enough sleep each night. In addition to these self-care fundamentals to support a healthy mind and body, it's also important to recognise when we need extra support. Especially when experiencing increased anxiety, overwhelm, or burnout, we need to be brave enough to speak out and seek professional help. It can be incredibly empowering to speak to a psychologist or counsellor and arm yourself with helpful strategies and new tools for your mental wellbeing toolkit.

I am regularly asked to share my strategies for managing stress and anxiety across my social media accounts. For those interested in learning more about the form of therapy I have used for the last seven years, I encourage you to look into EMDR (Eye Movement Desensitization and Reprocessing). It works on the premise that we can shift and reprocess past painful memories to move forward in life in a healthy way and undo old and unhealthy or unhelpful behavioural patterns. We become more aware of what has been unresolved and under the surface, and by dealing with these memories, we become less reactive and more responsive in our daily lives; this is especially true when working through memories that feel "sticky," emotionally charged, or traumatic. I added seeing a psychologist to my wellbeing toolkit when I was eighteen years old, and while I found it helpful to try techniques such as CBT (Cognitive Behavioural Therapy), EMDR has been the only model of treatment to effectively help me manage anxiety and truly bring about transformational and rapid positive change in my life. Remember, change happens when you're ready to change.

PART 5:

Reset for
a New Week

CHAPTER 13:

Preparing for a New Day

"Every new beginning comes from some other beginning's end."

–Seneca

I feel like congratulations are in order for making it to the final part of this book. This section is all about how to reset for a new day and week. While the focus of the first half of this book has been about how to begin and successfully execute your day, this final section is designed to help you end your day on a positive note and embrace a fresh start brought on by a new week. In the following chapters, you will discover best practices for how to wind down at the end of the day. As you've seen, rest is essential for our overall productivity, especially a good night's sleep. I'll take you through a step-by-step framework for designing your optimal night-time routine to successfully bookend your day and ensure you are well-rested. Your evenings are not just a way to unwind and energetically reset for a new day; they are an opportunity to prepare for the following morning. This is because a successful day starts the night before. Your night routine is your opportunity to mindfully plan for tomorrow, so you can wake up feeling ready to take on the day and avoid the

stress and rush of the morning that we otherwise risk facing.
You'll discover simple yet essential habits to build into your
evenings to support your mornings and set you up for another
successful day. Finally, this section concludes with a series of
powerful exercises and prompts to help you mindfully reflect on
the week and make any necessary adjustments for how you will
approach a new week. I encourage you to continue to review your
routines, schedule, responsibilities, and commitments and be an
active editor of your life. Life is dynamic and ever-changing, and so
are our needs. Only when we consciously take stock and actively
readjust our approach to daily life can we find our flow state and
build a life of success.

Only over the last few years have I begun to prioritise my night
routine and build little rituals that help me unwind and reset for a
new day. I've always had some form of night routine (e.g., brush
my teeth, wash off my makeup, and watch a show before bed),
but my appreciation for my night routine and the role it plays in
both the quality of my sleep and how organised I am when I wake
up the following morning is something I've only recently begun to
cultivate. I credit my new and improved routine to my regular morning
yoga classes and my commitment to working from a coworking
space several days a week. I need my mornings to be easy breezy,
stress-free, and streamlined so I can leave the house on time and
feel on top of my day. The last thing I want is to be rushing to get
myself organised or lacking clear direction for the day's focus. As I
previously mentioned, your night routine *bookends* your day. I like to
use my evenings to tie up any loose ends, prepare for the following
morning, and spend time relaxing with my husband Adam and our
dog Winston and having a little quiet time to myself.

Here's a look at my current night routine during the week:

* We usually sit down to eat dinner together around 7:00 p.m. I like to put on a playlist such as "Dinner Jazz" or "Dinner Mood" and light some candles to create a calming atmosphere. (We started playing music and lighting candles during our state's lockdowns throughout 2020–2021 and have kept it up ever since.)

* After dinner, I prepare my breakfast and organise my lunch to take to work. When I have the time and motivation to meal prep on a Sunday, preparing my lunch during the week is as simple as setting aside some fruit, crackers, and one of my favourite choc-peanut butter protein bliss balls to go along with whatever I've prepared in one of the containers in the fridge.

* I then pick out my clothes for the following day, usually my workout clothes for yoga and something to change into afterwards when I'm at the office. This saves me a lot of time in the morning and stops me from procrastinating and plodding in my pyjamas too long.

* I always make it a habit to pack my bag the night before. I go through my mental checklist and pack my laptop, laptop charger, headphones, reading glasses, and notebook. I also have an alarm that goes off in the mornings so I don't run late for yoga, and it also reminds me to pack my lunch that I keep in the fridge overnight. Another trick is to leave your keys in the fridge with your food, so you don't leave the house without your lunch. (Thanks, Mum, for the handy tip!)

* I like to consult my diary in the evenings, so I know what I have planned for the next day. Sometimes I'll look over it at the end of my work session, although I usually check it in the evening. This helps to remind me of my work focus for the following day, so I can wake up and already know how I plan to spend my time.

* Later in the evening is usually when I like to have a shower. While some people prefer to shower in the mornings, I mostly

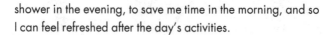

shower in the evening, to save me time in the morning, and so I can feel refreshed after the day's activities.

✱ I like to do my evening skincare, which is as simple as cleanse, wash, apply serum, and moisturise. If I didn't wear makeup that day, which is about 50 percent of the time, I sometimes skip this step in my night-time routine simply because I can't always be bothered. (Thought I should be honest.) I'm sure as I get older, I will prioritise it more.

✱   After that, it's time for pyjamas, herbal tea (with the occasional small snack), and sometimes some light reading before cuddling up on the couch with Adam and Winston to watch a show.

✱   I should also mention that I try not to spend much time on my phone in the evenings and steer clear of social media or the news during this time of day. It makes it a lot easier for me to unwind since I'm not trying to fill my mind with more information, news, or negativity.

✱   I wrap up my night routine with puppy pats on the bed until I give Winston the command to hop into his bed. His current bed of choice at night is our armchair in the bedroom, although he plays a game of musical chairs and will move across multiple areas during the night, including underneath our bed, his bed in the living room, my side of the bed, Adam's feet, and sometimes one of the pillows next to the bed that I throw onto the ground when I am ready to go to sleep.

Here's a mini summary of my night routine:

- ✓   Dinner
- ✓   Prepare breakfast and lunch
- ✓   Pick out clothes
- ✓   Pack my bag
- ✓   Check my diary
- ✓   Shower

- ✓ Skincare
- ✓ Couch time with Adam and Winston
- ✓ Puppy pats
- ✓ Lights out

To help you prepare for the following morning, I've also put together a suggested evening checklist:

- ✱ Prepare your breakfast and lunch the night before

- ✱ Pack your bag with all your necessary items

- ✱ Set your alarms for the following morning (e.g., "wake up," "go to gym," "pack lunch," etc.)

- ✱ Choose and lay out your clothes

- ✱ Check your schedule for tomorrow

- ✱ Spend five to ten minutes tidying up the house and putting things away

In addition to preparing for a new day, your night routine is there to facilitate a good night's sleep. It's your opportunity to build in some of the little acts of self-care we've previously discussed and use the time to relax, unwind, and restore your energy. Sleep is the number one underlying pillar of our health. Unlike nutrition, fitness, and mental wellbeing, which all act as contributing partners to our health, sleep forms the foundation of our health and wellbeing. It's therefore essential that we prioritise our sleep and do what we can to support a night of deep sleep by practising good sleep hygiene. Sleep hygiene refers to various habits and practices that regularly help us have good sleep quality and feel alert in the daytime. This includes not just the things we do, eat, drink, and watch, but also our external environments, such as the amount of light our eyes are exposed to, noise, and even the cleanliness and temperature of the room. Practising good sleep hygiene as part of our nightly routine is essential. Regular poor sleep can put you at an increased risk of numerous serious health conditions, including diabetes, obesity, and coronary heart disease. I was shocked to read that those with insomnia are ten times more likely to have depression and seventeen times more likely to have an anxiety disorder.[5] These are concerning findings and emphasise the need for us to prioritise sleep and no longer continue working late hours at the expense of a good night's rest. Getting enough quality sleep each night is essential for a long and healthy life.

Before sharing my list of helpful tips and tricks for a good night's sleep and my favourite rituals to build into your night routine, I first wanted to flag the main don'ts associated with poor sleep hygiene. These are things that you might currently do that seem harmless but can jeopardise your ability to fall asleep shortly after you go to bed and the quality of your sleep. I urge you to consider whether you are currently participating in any of these behaviours and replace them with healthier habits.

* **Exposure to blue light:** Spending the later hours of your day with your eyes glued to your phone, tablet, TV, or laptop further subjects your eyes to bright lights and harmful blue LED light. Bright light exposure represses feelings of sleepiness by disrupting our circadian rhythm and the brain's melatonin production—a necessary hormone for sleep. This is why you might find it hard to feel sleepy when watching a show in bed or scrolling on your phone late at night. Blue LED light has also been found to increase the production of the stress hormone cortisol by more than 50 percent. This can lead to restlessness, anxiety, and feeling "wired" or mentally unable to switch

---

5   A 2005 study by Taylor et al. found people with insomnia had greater depression and anxiety levels than people not having insomnia and were 9.82 and 17.35 times as likely to have clinically significant depression and anxiety, respectively. Increased insomnia frequency was related to increased depression and anxiety, and increased number of awakenings was also related to increased depression.

off.[6] I can relate to these side effects. Whenever I've spent too much time on my devices in the evening (and even during the day), I can feel overstimulated and my mind feels too full to decompress. The increased exposure to harmful blue LED light from our screens has led to the development of blue-light blocking glasses to protect our eyes. I've recently come across several brands on Instagram that supply these glasses and I think it's a fantastic and much-needed invention. There's also a night-time setting available on iPad and iPhone that dims the screen and changes the light to a warmer yellow tone that is gentler on the eyes. I wouldn't say these solutions make it okay to be on your devices late at night, but they help to mitigate the effects of bright light and blue LED light.

* **Cluttered environment:** A messy room could also be keeping you up at night. Cluttered rooms can make it harder to fall asleep because the environment can make you feel restless, as it hardly screams calm and peaceful. It's especially difficult if you keep lots of work, handouts, textbooks, stationery, and your laptop nearby and on display. If you have a desk in your room, aim to pack up your work before bedtime so it's out of sight and out of mind. I also encourage you to spend a couple of minutes each evening tidying up your room before you go to bed.

* **Inconsistent sleep and wake times:** Having consistent sleep and wake times is vital to our overall wellbeing. Going to bed at different times and sometimes staying up late into the early morning can throw off your body's natural circadian rhythm or internal clock. When you establish a consistent sleep schedule, your internal clock can reliably produce the right hormones necessary for a good night's sleep. If you usually go to sleep at 10:00 p.m., then your brain is trained to release

---

6 Leproult and colleagues looked at the effect of bright light exposure on the production of hormones known to be affected by sleep deprivation or involved in the production and activation or cortisol.

melatonin around this time each evening to help you feel
sleepy. When you throw off your usual sleep schedule and
start going to bed later some nights, your brain holds off on
the release of melatonin and can't predict when you will likely
be going to bed and when you need to gradually begin to
feel drowsy.

* **Insufficient sleep:** While the recommendation is that we
  aim for eight hours of sleep each night, so that we feel alert
  and able to focus the next day, some of us need more sleep
  and others need less. If you wake up feeling tired and find
  it hard to stay alert during the day or need a nap, you likely
  need more sleep. I'm a nine-hours kind of gal.

With the dreadful don'ts of sleep hygiene out of the way, I thought I'd
share my top five tips to help you fall asleep more easily. These are
habits that you can implement to help you achieve quality sleep each
night and feel refreshed the following morning.

1. **Try an evening wind-down.** If you notice that you're
   spending too much time on your phone in the evenings, this
   is a great way to set some healthy boundaries and help your
   mind relax. Currently, I enjoy the "Wind Down" guided
   meditation on the Balance app. It's a five-minute exercise
   where you place your finger on the screen and follow the
   moving circle, pairing each inhale as it moves to one side
   and each exhale as it moves to the other. At the end of the
   meditation, you're encouraged to put your phone away for
   the rest of the evening to signal to your mind that it's time to
   get ready for bed. You might like to try it or create your own
   wind-down ritual, such as taking an evening walk, making a
   tea, or journaling, and commit to putting away your phone
   afterwards. To hold yourself accountable, try setting an alarm
   on your phone and labelling it with positive benefits such as
   "Phone down. Sleep better. Feel calm." I encourage you to
   try scheduling an alarm on your phone for one hour before

you plan to go to bed to help reduce excessive and late-night digital consumption.

2. **Sleep in a dark room.** I find it hard to fall asleep unless my bedroom is pitch black. It can be tricky if you also share a bed with a partner who likes staying up later than you. The consensus is that the darker the room, the better. This is also why they make window covers for kids' rooms, to help block light and stop children and babies from waking up mid-nap. The test is to hold up your hand in front of your face and if you can still see it with the lights out, the room isn't dark enough yet. You can also sleep with an eye mask if you can't get your room dark enough.

3. **Diffuse lavender oil.** Lavender essential oil is a great way to help reduce stress and promote feelings of calm in the evenings. I like to only use certified organic lavender oil, so that I know it's the purest and the highest quality. When my sister moved back home from London a couple of years ago, she bought me a little bottle of pure organic English lavender oil that smells heavenly. For a while, I would carry it around in my handbag, but now I keep it on the shelf in the dining room next to our diffuser.

4. **Try a natural sleep supplement.** Numerous natural sleep supplements on the market contain different minerals and herbs, such as magnesium, valerian, passionflower, and ashwagandha. I've tried several of these and found some worked better than others. Magnesium seems to be the most widely used to promote relaxation and a good night's sleep. I take a magnesium supplement once daily and have for the past four years, as it's also vital for supporting female hormonal health. If you're keen to incorporate a supplement to help you sleep, consult your healthcare practitioner first, especially if you have any pre-existing health conditions. It's

important to make sure it's right for you and that you take the correct dosage.

5. **Meditate:** Meditation is another excellent way to relax the mind and body before bed. Try a guided meditation or listen to a relaxing playlist as you close your eyes and focus on slowing down and deepening your breath for five to ten minutes in the evenings. You might also like to practise one of my favourite restorative yoga poses I shared earlier and rest your legs up the wall for five to ten minutes while supporting your lower back with a folded blanket, cushion, or bolster. This yoga pose is said to be great for promoting deep sleep, as so many yoga teachers have told me over the years.

The Do's and Don'ts of a Night Routine:

Don't	Do
Drink caffeine in the evenings	Drink herbal teas such as chamomile or lemongrass and ginger
Eat processed sugars in the evenings that spike your blood sugar	Eat whole foods and foods known to help promote a good night's sleep, such as bananas, almonds, and oatmeal
Fall asleep next to your phone	Place your phone out of reach, ideally outside the bedroom
Forget to schedule your sleep	Go to bed at a similar time each night to build a regular sleep schedule

Use your phone, TV, or laptop up until you fall asleep	Set a screen-time alarm an hour before bed for when you will put your devices away
Eat right before bed	Prioritise eating a substantial dinner and aim to finish eating and snacking two hours before you go to sleep to let your digestive system rest overnight
Sleep with lights on	Sleep in a pitch-black room. Use a sleep mask, turn off all lights, and make sure your blinds block out streetlights
Sleep in a cluttered or messy room	Create a calming and tidy sanctuary for sleep

Here are twenty evening rituals you might like to build into your night routine to help you relax and unwind:

Bubble bath	Skincare routine	Read ten pages of your book
Listen to a relaxing playlist	Diffuse lavender oil	Wear comfy pyjamas
Journal	List three things that made you smile today	Watch a comedy show or something light-hearted

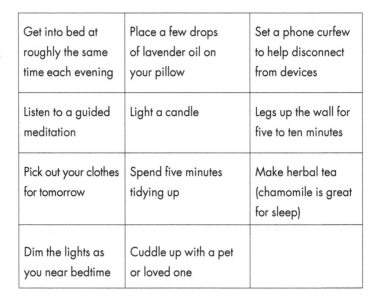

Get into bed at roughly the same time each evening	Place a few drops of lavender oil on your pillow	Set a phone curfew to help disconnect from devices
Listen to a guided meditation	Light a candle	Legs up the wall for five to ten minutes
Pick out your clothes for tomorrow	Spend five minutes tidying up	Make herbal tea (chamomile is great for sleep)
Dim the lights as you near bedtime	Cuddle up with a pet or loved one	

An Activity to Spark Action:

Scan over the table containing twenty evening rituals and circle any that appeal to you. Next, use the following spaces to create a night-time routine and incorporate as many of these rituals as you like. You may want to include additional rituals not presented in the table. Use the timestamps as a helpful guide to plan out your evening.

* Remember, when it comes to habit formation, writing your goals significantly increases your likelihood of accomplishing them. By taking a few minutes here to write down what your ideal night-time routine looks like to you, you're increasing your chances of successfully implementing these new daily habits.

Here's an example of a section of my night-time routine:

* 7:00 p.m. Dinner with Adam (light candles, listen to relaxing playlist, no phones on table)

* 7:30 p.m. Prepare breakfast and lunch for the following day

* 7:45 p.m. Pick out my clothes for tomorrow and pack my bag for work

* 8:00 p.m. Shower

___p.m._____

_____

___p.m. _____

_____

___p.m. _____

_____

___p.m. _____

_____

___p.m. _____

_____

___p.m. _____

_____

___p.m. _____

_____

___p.m. _____

_____

___p.m. _____

_____

___p.m. _____

_____

___p.m. _____

_____

Remember to be flexible and accept that your night routine may
change throughout the year, so you will need to adjust your schedule
or plan accordingly. My night routine changes with the seasons,
and I tend to opt for more cosy rituals during the colder months, like
making hot cocoa, taking a bath or long hot shower, and curling
up with a hot water bottle and flipping through cookbooks or home
décor magazines. I've recently started to set an alarm for 8:00 p.m.
to remind me to stretch, which is a new habit I'm trying to keep up
this year. So long as your night-time routine is helping you to prepare
for the following day and promote a good night's sleep, that's
what's important.

CHAPTER 14:

Weekly Reset

"Without reflection, we go blindly on our way, creating more unintended consequences, and failing to achieve anything useful."

–Margaret J. Wheatley

Why do people love celebrating New Year's Eve? I believe it's because a new year symbolises a fresh start. Even the first day of a new month or the first day of a new week can feel refreshing and make us believe that our slate has been wiped clean again. The problem is these dates that we flag as special or unique don't have any magical powers. Just because it's a new year doesn't mean things will be different. Just because it's Monday doesn't mean this week will be better than the last. This is because nothing changes if nothing changes. While these dates don't change anything, they can act as reminders to take stock and reflect on the previous week, month, or year. I say, let them be important invitations for reflection and active change. Reflection is key to living a successful life because it brings our attention to what's working and what's not.

Since awareness is the first step towards change, tuning into your body and becoming more conscious of how you allocate your time and energy puts you in a position of power. Many people, unfortunately, are in a state of perpetual doing and don't take time to pause and reflect on their behaviours or question how they can improve their lives. Some people even use their busy schedules to suppress the cries of their bodies and push past exhaustion until burnout strikes. We don't need to wait until we are bedridden to listen to our body's wisdom. We can invite a moment of solitude each week and get curious about what's working and what's not. When we take a step back to notice whether life supports our priorities and wellbeing, we can adjust accordingly. The more conscious we become of our behaviours and the better we get at tuning into our bodies, the sooner we can pick up on any unhealthy tendencies, habits, and thoughts and make a change for the better.

Remember, life is dynamic, and our needs and responsibilities are always changing. Work-life balance is not a box we check off once. It's a way of living that requires us to be the active editors of our own lives. As you start to feel the boat rock and tip in one direction (perhaps too much time working), practise the art of awareness and pick up on your behaviours, patterns, and tendencies that have left you feeling burnt out, stressed, or overwhelmed in the past. Like I said at the beginning, this book is not about being perfect because that's unrealistic and I'm not about promoting unattainable standards that don't factor in the complexities of life. It's not about adhering to your routines and schedules with the expectation that you'll never veer off track or find yourself needing to adjust. I expect you to stray from your routines from time to time because you're human and need to (and *should*) refine and adjust as you go because life is unpredictable. Some weeks will unavoidably be more busy or stressful than others and call for more self-care to help replenish your energy. I intend

to help you smooth out the bumps along the way and equip you with the tools to protect your wellbeing so you don't burn out or feel overwhelmed. It's misleading to think that because we've written down our schedules, our lives will forever be perfectly organised and that it's smooth sailing from here on out. While routines protect our mental and physical wellbeing, there may still be times when we feel stressed, anxious, sad, or exhausted due to unexpected curveballs and challenges that life throws our way.

The exercises and prompts throughout this chapter are here to help you gain awareness of your behaviours and situations and identify the necessary changes that you need to implement to create a more supportive lifestyle that facilitates deeper productivity, self-care, and intentional living.

As you make your way through this final chapter, I'll share several key questions I ask myself at the end of each week when doing my weekly reset. These questions will help you identify any changes you need to implement to better support and honour yourself the following week. We'll also plan for a new week together so that you can confidently set yourself up for a productive and positive week, all while making sure to account for your top priorities. Finally, you'll discover how to best approach those times when you feel out of balance to bring yourself back into the driver's seat and successfully navigate these moments to get yourself back on track.

> **"I discovered that a fresh start is a process. A fresh start is a journey–a journey that requires a plan."**
>
> **–Vivian Jokotade**

Weekly Reset:
Journal Prompts for the End
of Each Week

I invite you to use the following journaling prompts for your weekly reset. These prompts will help you become aware of where you are allocating your time and energy most. They will also help you tune into your body and identify how you're feeling after the week. As you complete these prompts, you will notice what's working and what's not. Use this newfound awareness to inform your actions and workload for the following week and make any adjustments.

Reflect on the major things that you achieved this week. Create an "I Did It" list to remind yourself how you spent your time and energy and everything you asked of your mind and body.

_____

_____

_____

_____

_____

_____

Reflect on what went well this week. What good things happened to you? Write your weekly gratitudes in the space below.

_____

_____

_____

_____

_____

_____

Body check-in: How do you feel in your body after last week? Tired? Energised? Irritable? Happy? Optimistic? What messages can you receive from your body if you take a moment to listen?

_____

_____

_____

_____

_____

_____

Is there anything that needs changing? Think about what you
would like to do more/less of in this coming week.

_____

_____

_____

_____

_____

_____

How can you nurture and nourish yourself this week?

_____

_____

_____

_____

_____

_____

Set an intention for the coming week.

_____

 _____

Planning for a New Week

I find it helpful to plan out my week in advance and schedule
any commitments, responsibilities, and tasks before the busyness
sets in. Approaching my week this way helps ensure that the most
important things are always accounted for. It also gives me a sense of
clarity and control over my week. I encourage you to follow the steps
below and plan your week to ensure a healthy balance and keep you
on track. You can do this at the end of the week, whether it's a few
minutes in the morning, afternoon, or before bed. What's important is
that you set aside some time to organise your schedule before a new
week begins. I like to spend time on a Sunday afternoon booking my
yoga and Pilates classes for the week, scheduling time for self-care
(like taking myself out for a chai latte and to the park at 2:00 p.m. on
Monday after I finish my writing session), scheduling any new to-dos
for the week and blocking out time to work on my various projects.

My top five not-to-miss steps when planning for a new week:

- ✓ Schedule time for exercise
- ✓ Make time for self-care and rest
- ✓ Schedule all upcoming to-dos

✓   Block out time for projects, assignments, and other major
     work/study commitments
     ✓ Set yourself a daily top priority

Getting Back on Track

The unpredictable nature of life, coupled with the many challenges
and lessons that get placed in our path, means veering off track is
something we all experience at times. The issue is not whether we
veer off track and, to an extent, stray from our routines. The issue is
how quickly we identify that we have strayed from what helps build
structure, support, and sustainability into our lifestyle and how easily
we can move back into alignment.

In 2020 and 2021, I veered off track and wasn't feeling like my
usual happy self. My mornings were far less productive than usual,
and my work routine blurred into the rest of my day. This change in
my approach to life was brought on by several extended lockdowns
in my state, where I couldn't go far from my house for months at a
time. Fortunately for me, I had the support of my family and friends,
psychologist, life coach, and spiritual counsellor. I call them my
support trifecta. I have learned that it's not whether we fall to our
knees that determines our inner strength but how quickly we get
back up. In those moments, I let myself experience the pain, sadness,
anger, and grief that came with navigating a pandemic and multiple
lockdowns. I also quickly reached out for help and spoke up. The
support and guidance of the people around me help me through
difficult times and remind me that I'm not alone and that I don't
always need to have all the answers, but I do need to be willing
to meet myself where I am and be proactive to help myself get
back on track.

I share this because I want you to understand that you won't always feel happy, productive, motivated, focused, and energised. I don't expect you to. I expect you to be human and give yourself permission to feel the ebb and flow of life. I want you to release expectations of perfection and this constant state of productivity and instead, acknowledge that life is a constant act of falling out of and bringing yourself back into a state of alignment. You might experience this dance in the presence of a breakup, loss, grief, birth, or any other significant life event. Starting a new job or taking on a new project can also bring about some turbulence in your daily life and you might find yourself straying from your usual routine. That's okay. This book is here to give you the framework, tools, and advice to create these routines to optimise your day and help you get back on track with some necessary self-compassion. You can always reschedule, edit, and revise as life changes. It's the framework that's important.

So what can you do when you veer off track and things don't go as planned? There are four steps to getting back on track that have proven particularly helpful each time life rocked my boat and I felt a little or completely off-balance.

This process encourages you to reflect and do so with love, identify your supports, and effectively edit and adjust accordingly.

* **Reflect:** It's important to notice what's been happening recently in your life and identify any major life changes, disruptions, or added responsibilities. This is where your weekly reset and the journaling prompts provided earlier in this chapter will help you become aware of your "why."

* **With love:** Practise self-compassion and acknowledge that you're human. As a result, we all experience hiccups, setbacks, and challenges that we need to face and overcome.

That's simply part of life but you can and will get through it. There's no use beating yourself up if you find yourself overworking and burnt out, procrastinating and falling behind, or skipping your morning workouts or daily meditation. Identify what's happened, acknowledge where you are, and use it to inform how you'll move forward.

* **Identify your supports:** Your support network is your greatest asset in life. If you have a great psychologist, life coach, counsellor, or mentor, make sure to reach out for added support to help you get back into your routines and feel like your best self as soon as possible. Maybe your support network includes colleagues, teachers, family, or friends. Perhaps you have a great GP or naturopath you can reach out to if you're concerned about your wellbeing. Whether you notice yourself feeling anxious, stressed, and overwhelmed, feeling physically drained and emotionally flat, or you're placing too much pressure on yourself, know that you don't have to navigate these challenges alone. I can't stress enough how important it is to seek help and confide in the people you trust whenever life gets tough. There have been times when increased anxiety has made it hard to get my work done. Then there were times when I found myself lacking direction in my work life and needing clarity to move forward. This is where my supports come in.

  ✧ Side note, as I am writing this section, I just hit play on my playlist and the song it landed on (it's set to shuffle) is called "A Little Help." Perhaps it's a sign? I'll let you decide.

* **Edit:** The last step I want you to do is to make some necessary changes. Like I said earlier, nothing changes if nothing changes. What needs changing in your life so that you can feel more supported, energised, and focused, to show up as your best self? This is your invitation to start fresh and head back to the drawing board and think about a manageable

plan to help you get back on track. This may be something you work on with your support network. For example, I often write down my action plan while speaking with my psychologist or life coach. One thing I will stress is to make sure to write down your plan as though you are writing a commitment to yourself. Having it written and displayed or building these changes into your diary so that your schedule reflects your plan for getting back on track will help hold you accountable and bring you peace of mind.

I invite you to incorporate the prompts provided throughout this chapter into your weekly reset. When you reflect on each week, you're able to move mindfully into a new week with greater intention and the awareness of how to best meet your needs and the responsibilities and demands of your work life. You might like to make this part of your night-time routine on a Sunday evening or set aside some time during the day to complete the reflective exercises. You could even answer them together with your partner, family, or friend, as part of your weekly debrief. I'll leave it to you to choose how you answer these questions. What I want most for you to take away from this chapter are the benefits that come with taking a pause at the end of a week. By cultivating a more curious, introspective, and proactive approach to life, you will also be able to draw on these tendencies to help you move back into alignment with your lifestyle when you veer off track and to do so more quickly, and importantly, while feeling more supported.

Please know that you can also revisit this chapter, along with the rest, anytime. Remember, you are the editor of your life, but you don't have to do it alone.

To the Reader...

I hope you will use the lessons and teachings found throughout this book to help you navigate the many challenges, unexpected surprises, and exciting moments of life. May the messages in this book find their way into your daily life and bring you a newfound sense of clarity and calm. May these chapters leave you feeling empowered to take control of your life in this busy and noisy world and inspire you to be gentle with yourself. Thank you for allowing me to be part of your journey and share my stories and wisdom with you. I am filled with gratitude and humbled by this opportunity to play even a small role in supporting you, your ambitions, and the wonderful life you are creating.

With love,
Jessica

Acknowledgements

I am deeply grateful for all the people in my life who continue to support my work, believe in me, and enrich my life. Writing this book has been made possible because of the incredible support network around me.

A huge and very deserving thank you to Hugo, my editor at Mango Publishing, for guiding me through this process. You're a pleasure to work with, both on my first book, *The High School Survival Guide*, and now my second book. I am deeply thankful for your ongoing support and encouragement, and your belief in this book and your initial excitement in the way this idea came about.

Thank you to Christopher McKenney for creating the best publishing house out there that gives creators like me the opportunity to share our message through our love of writing.

To the wider team at Mango, thank you for helping to put this book together and for the ongoing work you do to support my first book, *The High School Survival Guide*, which is now a bestseller. Special mention to Minerve, Geena and Hannah from the Mango marketing team, who have worked hard to support both my literary works. Thank you to Elina for your wonderfully creative efforts in taking my initial ideas for the cover of this book and turning them into the finished design. I also want to give a mention to Meloni, Mango's head of developmental editing. Your detailed notes and feedback on the first draft of this book were incredibly helpful and pushed me to become a better writer. I deeply appreciate your input, which has helped make this book the incredible resource it is today.

I also want to thank one of Mango's newest members, and International Head of Publishing Director, Lou Johnson. Lou, you have made me feel supported throughout this entire experience and I'm delighted that you are now part of the Mango team. Thank you for always cheering me on, liking and commenting on my social media "book update" posts, and always making yourself available if ever I need you. Your warmth and encouragement have meant so much to me.

Thank you to my amazing videographers and editors, James and Jai, from Purpose Productions. You are an integral part of my team, and I am grateful to have worked together on my book announcement video. Thank you for helping me share my message with the world.

Josh Zimmerman, I am forever grateful for your ongoing support. Thank you for helping guide me through the challenges that come with being a digital creator and running my own business. You came into my life at precisely the right time. The work you do is invaluable to my business and wellbeing, and I have had countless "ah-ha" moments throughout our sessions.

Yvette Rae, your work has made a lasting and positive impact on my life, and I know that the guidance, support, and advice you have given me in my personal life have contributed to the ability to also be my best self in my business. Thank you from the bottom of my heart.

Evelynne Joffe, for helping me navigate my twenties and now early thirties. You helped me as I took a leap of faith into the unknown and began my business seven years ago and continue to support and provide guidance and awareness so that I can live in alignment and create a life that I truly love. Thank you for providing a safe space to air my worries when I have felt lost and for helping to steer me back on track.

A big thank you to Shannah Kennedy. Your written work has inspired me for years and I am so grateful for your review of this book. Thank you for taking the time to help support my work and for your encouragement over the years. It's been wonderful to have connected both online and in person with you!

To my dear friend Amanda Rootsey, I am so thankful that our paths crossed four years ago. You inspire everyone around you to live gently, including me. The way in which you live your life is a constant reminder to us all to be more self-compassionate and claim our right to rest. Thank you for your ongoing support and for providing a testimonial for the book.

Thank you to my yoga teacher Pru. This book is an example of how just a one-minute conversation about the struggles of sitting down to work can plant a seed of inspiration and grow into an entirely new resource for the world. Too often we forget how powerful a short exchange between two people can be. You asked me for my advice to help overcome your productivity and motivation blocks when it comes to sitting down to write your thesis for your master's degree. I hope this book is everything you need to help get you into the work zone. Thank you for also creating such a beautiful and calming space to recentre and allow my mind, body, and soul the time they need to recharge.

Thank you to my beautiful friends for always taking a genuine interest in my work and being so supportive, encouraging and selflessly excited for me and my wins. A special mention to Penny, Lanz, Natalie, Zara, Jessica O., and Jess M., for regularly checking in to see how the writing was progressing and for also giving your input and suggestions for potential titles for this book. A double thank you goes to Jess M, who runs Freshly Snapped Photography, for taking such beautiful photos of my work and all my photos for social media and my blog.

To all my extended family and family-in-law for the special relationships we share that bring meaning to my life and for your genuine interest and support in my work. A special mention to my parents-in-law, Tanya and Nathan. Your initial excitement as I shared my idea for this book over lunch while we spent the day in Somers meant so much to me. Nathan, I cherish the memory as we walked down the beach that afternoon and you mentioned your enthusiasm for this book once again. To my two incredible, caring, and supportive brothers-in-law, Brad and Nick, thank you for your words of encouragement over the years, the interest you take in my work, and the belief in what I do. Nick, I savour your birthday messages and reading that my work inspires you! Another special mention to Ros Ben-Moshe for being the incredibly proud and enthusiastic aunt that has taught me to always share my success and helped me to be proud of my achievements. I am grateful for your ongoing love and support!

To my parents, Dalia and Peter, I couldn't ask for more supportive, proud, and loving parents. Thank you for everything you have done for our family to give me the best life. Your support has been integral

to my success over the past seven years of my career, not to mention in becoming the person I am today. I love and appreciate you both so much.

To my sister Michelle, I am so blessed to have a sister and a best friend in you. Thank you for always being my proud sister and being so excited and over the moon for me. I am honoured to know that I inspire you in life. Also, thank you for the wonderfully stimulating phone conversations and book recommendations that helped inspire my work.

To my soul mate, teammate, husband, and best friend, Adam. Thank you for everything. Thank you for every time you have reassured me when I found myself worrying, being the voice of reason and compassion when I was too hard on myself, but most of all, thank you for always loving me unconditionally and bringing your happy energy into our home. I am so grateful to have a partner who beams with pride and jumps at the chance to talk about my accomplishments.

Finally, thank you to you, the reader. In reading this book, you allow me to continue to fulfil my dream of helping to support and guide people to create a happy and productive life they love.

About the Author

Jessica Holsman is a bestselling author, content creator, entrepreneur, and professional speaker. Jess is best known online for her planning and productivity tips, and work-life balance and wellbeing advice. With over 27 million views on her YouTube channel, *Study With Jess*, Jess continues to harness the power of social media to help her community increase their productivity, boost their mental health, and bring about long-lasting success. Jess is also the founder of the first-ever study stationery line for students, Educationery, and the bestselling author of the internationally successful study skills book, *The High School Survival Guide*. Jess's extensive experience in producing high-quality, impact-driven digital content has led to successful partnerships with Google, Screen Australia, and Screen Queensland, whereby she has since released two web series, *Life of Jess* and *MindFull*. She has also formed numerous partnerships with major globally renowned organisations, including Netflix, Adobe, ASUS, Sennheiser, and LG. Jess is also an internationally sought-after speaker, presenting for organisations including Adobe and VidCon.

Let's stay connected!
@studywithjess | Instagram
Study With Jess | Facebook
Youtube.com/StudyWithJess | YouTube
www.studywithjess.com

Share your favourite moments from this book and tag me
@StudyWithJess on Instagram!

References

Chapter 1

IDC. "Always Connected: How Smartphones and Social Keep Us Engaged." 2013. https://www.nu.nl/files/IDC-Facebook%20 Always%20Connected%20(1).pdf.

Mazza, Emilia. "Put the phone down! Wellness expert reveals what REALLY happens to our brain when we look at the screen first thing in the morning." *Daily Mail.com*. January 6, 2019. https://www. dailymail.co.uk/femail/article-6561617/Chelsea-Pottenger-checking-phone-wake-ruining-brain.html.

McRaven, William H. *Make Your Bed: Little Things That Can Change Your Life... And Maybe the World*. London: Grand Central Publishing, 2017.

Sharma, Robin. *Life Lessons from the Monk Who Sold His Ferrari*, 2nd ed. New York: Harper Collins, 2013.

Sharma, Robin. *The 5 AM Club*, 2nd ed. New York: HarperCollins, 2020.

Thomée, Sara, Annika Härenstam, and Mats Hagberg. "Mobile Phone Use and Stress, Sleep Disturbances, and Symptoms of

Depression among Young Adults - a Prospective Cohort Study."
BMC Public Health 11 (2011). https://doi.org/10.1186/1471-
2458-11-66.

Chapter 2

McKeown, Greg. *Essentialism: The Disciplined Pursuit of Less.*
New York: Crown Business, 2014.

Newport, Cal. *Deep Work.* New York: Grand Central
Publishing, 2016.

Vitti, Alisa. *In the FLO: A 28-Day Plan Working with Your
Monthly Cycle to Do More and Stress Less.* London: HQ,
HarperCollins UK, 2020.

Chapter 6

Dean, Jeremy. "5 Most Common Side-Effects of Ritalin (the 'Study
Drug')." *PsyBlog.* May 18, 2017. https://www.spring.org.
uk/2017/05/5-common-side-effects-ritalin-study-drug.php.

Eyal, Nir, and Julie Li. *Indistractable: How to Control Your Attention
and Choose Your Life.* Dallas: BenBella Books, 2019.

Goldsmith, Marshall, and Mark Reiter. *Triggers: Behavior That
Last—Becoming the Person You Want to Be.* New York: Crown
Business, 2015.

Robison, Lisa S., Mala Ananth, Michael Hadjiargyrou, David
E. Komatsu, and Panayotis K. Thanos. "Chronic Oral
Methylphenidate Treatment Reversibly Increases Striatal
Dopamine Transporter and Dopamine Type 1 Receptor Binding
in Rats." *Journal of Neural Transmission* 124 (2017): 655–67.
https://doi.org/10.1007/s00702-017-1680-4.

Twenge, Jean M., and W. Keith Campbell. "Associations between
Screen Time and Lower Psychological Well-Being among Children
and Adolescents: Evidence from a Population-Based Study."
Preventive Medicine Reports 12, no. 12 (2018): 271–283.
https://doi.org/10.1016/j.pmedr.2018.10.003.

Chapter 7

Clear, James. *Atomic Habits: An Easy and Proven Way to Build
Good Habits and Break Bad Ones.* New York: Penguin Random
House, 2018.

Chapter 8

Foroux, Darius. "How Common Is Procrastination? A Study."
Medium: The Blog of Darius Foroux. July 4, 2019. https://
medium.com/darius-foroux/how-common-is-procrastination-a-
study-80869467c3f3.

Steel, Piers. "The nature of procrastination: A meta-analytic and
theoretical review of quintessential self-regulatory failure."
Psychological Bulletin 133 (2017): 65–94. https://doi.
org/10.1037/0033-2909.133.1.65.

Stefanski, Ron. "How Declining Attention Spans Impact Your Social Media." *Muck Rack.* July 14, 2020. https://muckrack.com/blog/2020/07/14/how-declining-attention-spans-impact-your-social-media.

Chapter 12

Nestor, James. *BREATH: The New Science of a Lost Art.* New York: Riverhead Books, 2020.

Tornberg, D.C.F., H. Marteus, U. Schedin, K. Alving, J.O.N. Lundberg, and E. Weitzberg. "Nasal and Oral Contribution to Inhaled and Exhaled Nitric Oxide: A Study in Tracheotomized Patients." *European Respiratory Journal* 19 (2002): 859–864. https://doi.org/10.1183/09031936.02.00273502.

Chapter 13

Burgess, Helen J., and Thomas A. Molina. "Home Lighting before Usual Bedtime Impacts Circadian Timing: A Field Study." *Photochemistry and Photobiology* 90, no. 3 (2018): 723–726. https://doi.org/10.1111/php.12241.

Leproult, Rachel, Egidio F. Colecchia, Mireille L'Hermite-Balériaux, and Eve Van Cauter. "Transition from Dim to Bright Light in the Morning Induces an Immediate Elevation of Cortisol Levels." *Journal of Clinical Endocrinology & Metabolism* 86, no. 1 (2001): 151–157. https://doi.org/10.1210/jcem.86.1.7102.

Taylor, Daniel J., Kenneth L. Lichstein, H. Heith Durrence, Brant
W. Reidel, and Andrew J. Bush. "Epidemiology of Insomnia,
Depression, and Anxiety." *Sleep* 28, no. 11(2005): 1457–
1464. https://doi.org/10.1093/sleep/28.11.1457.

Williams, Caroline. "How to Breathe Your Way to Better Memory
and Sleep." *New Scientist*. January 8, 2020. https://www.
newscientist.com/article/mg24532640-600-how-to-breathe-your-
way-to-better-memory-and-sleep/.

Mango Publishing, established in 2014, publishes an eclectic list of books by diverse authors—both new and established voices— on topics ranging from business, personal growth, women's empowerment, LGBTQ studies, health, and spirituality to history, popular culture, time management, decluttering, lifestyle, mental wellness, aging, and sustainable living. We were recently named 2019 *and* 2020's #1 fastest-growing independent publisher by *Publishers Weekly.* Our success is driven by our main goal, which is to publish high-quality books that will entertain readers as well as make a positive difference in their lives.

Our readers are our most important resource; we value your input, suggestions, and ideas. We'd love to hear from you—after all, we are publishing books for you!

Please stay in touch with us and follow us at:

Facebook: Mango Publishing
Twitter: @MangoPublishing
Instagram: @MangoPublishing
LinkedIn: Mango Publishing
Pinterest: Mango Publishing
Newsletter: mangopublishinggroup.com/newsletter

Join us on Mango's journey to reinvent publishing,
one book at a time.

CPSIA information can be obtained
at www.ICGtesting.com
Printed in the USA
JSHW041609090722
27802JS00004B/7

9 781642 509526